THE PROFANE IN SACRED ART

The Spirit of Art Criticism

Kathleen Whittaker

Cover design by Daniel Silva

Contact Kathleen Whittaker:

theprofaneinsacredart@yahoo.com

Printed in the United States of America

First Printing September2022

ISBN: 978-17370964-0-5

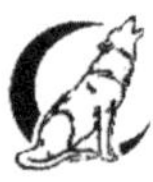

DEDICATION

This book is dedicated to all those artists, both known and unknown, throughout history, who worked solely for the glorification of God. Their work serves as an inspiration to those of us who are dedicated to creating works of sacred art in these dark, heretical times.

CONTENTS

Preface

"A time to be silent, a time to speak." (Eccl. 3:8). I can think of no better way to begin than to copy St. Theodore the Studite's beginning to *On the Holy Icons.*

Many who read this book may question my audacity in claiming the necessity for what may at first seem a new role for the clergy in the Church. That is, the role of 'art critic.' I have questioned it many times myself. After all, many may say, the Church was the *source* of Western art. We had high level sacred art in the Church before anybody saw the need for art critics. How can one suddenly say there is a need for art criticism in the Church? Surely, we can have good art without a 'critic?' Why bring this up as something new? Don't artists and the clergy just 'know' good art when they see it? Isn't there more 'religious art' being done today? These are all legitimate observations and questions that need to be addressed before I proceed. And that's without even mentioning that I also claim to know *how* to criticize art.

There are many lenses through which to view history. Many view it through politics, many through social institutions, and so on. As an artist I always viewed it through art. After being raised Catholic I left the Church as a teenager, largely because of Her (contemporary) attitude toward art. I could not believe that an institution that approved the production of such bad art could possibly be the guardian of Truth. I saw the great art of the past, but also saw that this was no more. It was through art that I left the Church, but it was also through art that I returned to Her.

When I became a stone carver, I experienced *unity* for the first time. *Unity*, as a formal, definite thing, not something I constructed, but something real, something objective. Not 'compromise,' not the 'merging' of different things giving parts of themselves up for the good of some 'whole,' but the development and growth of the different aspects of different things to the highest specific extent possible while at the same time fitting with something else, some other thing (or things) equally developed. The carving of over life-sized figures in marble, by hand, requires the utmost in physical work, along with the utmost in mental concentration (you cannot change what you have carved-without changing your idea). I began to realize that *this,* this unity between the physical and the non-physical, was the only vehicle for understanding and experiencing truth, because it is only through synthesis that one can be *prepared* for the experience of truth. Since God placed us in time and space with a soul, He must have given us the gift of a unified mind. Trying to think with synthesis, or coalescence, seemed the most basic, fundamental way to make the following of God's will possible. My journey through art to the Church had begun. Some questions that began to plague me were: *"What are the criteria upon which a priest accepts or rejects artwork for a church?"; "Why can't there be honest discussion concerning the quality of art in our churches?"; "Why can't one criticize religious art?"; "Why do I feel constantly caught between two worlds?" (There's serious art- i.e. secular-and then there's frivolous art-i.e. religious).* And the biggest elephant in the room: *"Why is contemporary art in the Church so bad, so un-sacred? What happened?"* But the knowledge that I received from the experience of unity remained. *This* was the characteristic of sacred art in the Church *before* the Renaissance-before the Protestant revolt.

Art can certainly be a vehicle for the truth, but it can equally be a vehicle for lies and untruth. Why was it commonly a vehicle for the truth (sacred) at one time and suddenly changed into a vehicle for untruth (un-sacred) at another (during the Renaissance) and could this be related in some way to the decline of the Church in our world? It had happened so fast. It was during the Renaissance that artists began choosing to separate and emphasize one thing at the expense of another, to eliminate from their work the unity so necessary for telling the truth. It's been in steep decline ever since. Is it possible that this could have helped pave the way for the Protestant revolt? Why, for example, was the expression of truth not included in the bases on which the value of a work of art rested?

I began to read everything I could find that showed the attitude of the Church toward art throughout history: Biblical texts, the writings of St John of Damascus and St Theodore the Studite, Church councils, papal encyclicals, papal letters. Two things emerged: 1) the making of images is inherently Catholic; and 2) the change in the hierarchy over time from the *experience* of art to the *theory* of art.

God loves images and wants us to make images (like He did); we may not even understand exactly why. The Church has taught the importance of images: iconoclasts are heretics. Is it therefore possible that these things can be true side by side with a reality in which there are *not* objective guidelines for the making of images? Has God ever left us in the lurch, keeping us in ignorance of how to please Him and letting us rely only on ourselves, on 'what we like'?

So, if there *were* objective rules to learn and follow in the making of works of art, it would follow that art criticism is possible, and perhaps, necessary. But where could I find these rules? They had to be something real, able to be described. The only discussions I could find set the whole subject in esoteric terms, which flew in the face of the universal significance of art. Because there was no real system of art criticism, where could I begin? How did the artists of the past make such *sacred* art? The only way I could think to begin was to look at myself as an artist. I resisted this for a long time because it seemed to conform to the very system I abhorred-one in which the artist's viewpoint was the determining factor in judging the work of art. But since I could find no concrete help, I hesitatingly began. I started by asking myself what the value of art was. If the value of art lies in telling the truth, then the true value of art had to lie in glorifying God, the Source of Truth. But how could an artist tell the truth, and therefore hope for success in glorifying God? It seemed too tall an order. So, the artist must, at the very least, face the duty of telling the small truths along the journey of his working. I began to question myself when working. What did I criticize as I was working? And why? What were the things I was trying to perfect? And why? What was the basis for deciding to change something or to do something differently? What was my response if I was tempted to take a shortcut, to take the easy way rather than the right way?

Five characteristics consistently emerged: *the idea, the composition, the level of technical expertise, the development of the work, and the conclusion of the work.* I compared them to the things I had experienced or read that were used as a basis for art criticism, sacred or not: *sincerity, fashion, style,* and *the place of the work in art history.* Strangely enough, the two lists did not intersect anywhere. The first thing to jump out was the *definite* nature of my list as opposed to the *indefinite* nature of the 'contemporary critics' list. This led me to dig deeper. Either I was wrong or the art critics were. Or was I missing something they saw and I didn't? In other words, was my list incomplete and if so, could these 'often used' bases of criticisms of a work of art be included within my own experience? So, I re-evaluated the things I thought essential to criticize in a work of art. If they were truly fundamental, and if art had universal importance, they would be reflected in God's revelations and creation. And yes, they were. Taking them one by one, there were intersections everywhere: in the Bible, in Church teaching, in nature. This was very exciting. The evaluation of the 'popular' bases for art criticism revealed no such thing. This 'other' list was simply not reflected substantially anywhere. Although characteristics on this list could be discussed in a work of art (and it could be of some interest to do so), on none of them did the quality of artistic merit depend. They were the *accidents* of a work of art, not the *essence.*

The challenge of selecting serious fine art for a church is simply not being met. Period. This seems due to a combination of two things: by a complete lack of the knowledge of what actually makes a good work of art, on the side of both the artist and the patron (the clergy), *and* by a general fear of criticizing religious art-both fruits of a dis-unified mind. Also, there seems to be a lack of the understanding that well executed art is essential, that putting good art in a church is *following God's will* and that accepting bad art is *against God's will.* As long as we take a superficial and conceptual attitude which severs the relationship between subject matter and criticism, we will never have good art.

So, I must speak. *"I am not forcing myself in where I have no right to act."* (St. Patrick's letter to Coroticus). I am not "forcing myself in" because I am already a part of this system. I am an artist who does religiously themed work and have done public work for Catholic churches. My "right to act" comes from the acceptance of my artistic responsibility, which is total. I accept my responsibility to answer questions and/or criticisms of my work, to not waste the viewer's time convincing him to like it, but to keep quiet and allow him his own reaction.

So called 'sacred' art in the Church today is anything but. In fact, the contemporary 'art' which is supposed to be sacred is so far from it that it is the cause of many leaving the path of Truth and *prevents* others from finding It. Something must be done. We are in a time of peril and must use methods perhaps so far unused, or used in a different way, in the Church. That's all I am suggesting. I am not injecting something 'new.' Art criticism did not exist formally in the Church in the past because there was no need. When both the artist and the clergy thought with a more unified mind, they were natural art critics: they knew the truth when they saw it. We do not.

It is of fundamental and supreme importance to have high quality artwork for the inside of our churches. But much work needs to be done. We must first realize that we have become participants in an anti-Catholic (anti-image) culture, then we must learn how to see, and we *must* learn how to criticize.

A Note on Terminology

<u>critic</u>: In this book the critic is, for the most part, assumed to be the member of the clergy who is responsible for placing the work of art in the church. It may also refer to the viewer. It does not mean a professional who is paid to analyze art.

<u>*history/story*</u>: These two words are used interchangeably. A story can either be true or an invention. In this book the history being referred to is also a story. It is a story that is true.

Introduction

The devout believer welcomes his duty to attend Sunday Mass. There can be nothing else in his life that has so strong a potential for the reception of the grace that will enable him to fulfill his destiny of becoming holy. To actively participate in the Holy Sacrifice of Our Lord, to receive the Body and Blood of Our Lord Himself, is an honor almost too great to comprehend. The physical environment in which the Mass is celebrated should reflect the greatness and solemnity of this event. When someone enters a church, he should be awed at the atmosphere of holiness. He should truly feel reminded of another level of existence. As much as possible he should feel in fact that he himself *is* entering another level of existence-because he is.

The church, simply as a building, has a multi-faceted duty. It should represent physical matter in its highest form and purpose, that of glorifying God and affirming the beauty of God's creation. All aspects of this physical environment should teach the truth. But these are not the only duties of the church building. As Pope Pius XII wrote in his encyclical *Musicae Sacrae,* architecture, painting and sculpture [in a church] *"serve to prepare a worthy setting for the sacred ceremonies."*

We know that the spiritual benefits of assisting at Holy Mass are greater or lesser according to the disposition of the individual. We also know that the "setting" is something which is either a help or a hindrance to our participation at Mass. We should also be aware that the vast majority of individuals are unaware of this power of the "setting." So, the purpose of a church is to give assistance or to be a help, both to the people attending Mass *and* the priest who is celebrating Mass. Since the purpose of the Mass is to help to lead people to their salvation, everything about as well as *in* the church building should lead to transformation through prayer. An atheist, walking into a Catholic church, should be overwhelmed with a sense of the enormity and power of the Catholic Idea.

Anyone can see that the quality of the art in our churches has been changing, declining in quality, for several hundred years. Many, if not most newly built churches in the United States do not even have original artwork at all; instead, they rely on mass produced copies of sacred images. Or, they have original 'artwork,' the acceptance of which seems to depend on how superficial and generic it is, on how closely it resembles something mass-produced. This raises some serious questions, such as *'Why is this?' How did this happen?'* And *'Does it matter?'* If it does matter-and the premise of this book is that it is of crucial importance-then the next question is *'Can we begin to change things?'* and if so, *'How?'*

The major premise of this book is that we *can begin* to change this state of affairs. It will be a long process, one that will extend far beyond our lifetimes. It is clear that artists have lost their way. The place to begin is with a serious, sustained art criticism from those responsible for placing art in the churches (the clergy), which is based not on 'conceptualism,' 'relativism,' 'evangelism,' or any other ideology, but simply on the truth of Trinitarian Reality.

This book is divided into several parts. In the first part we explore the Biblical roots of art as well as art in the history of the Church. This part contains much that will be familiar to the

Catholic, and as a result may seem self-evident. I urge the reader to take a deeper look and to meditate on what I have written. Although Catholics may say "Oh yes, I agree and I already know that", this cannot be true. It cannot be true because if it were, neither the Catholic clergy nor the laity would tolerate the bad and non-art that they see in their churches, let alone create it. The first part also discusses the proper mental attitude necessary in order to be able to look at a work of art objectively.

The second part is the 'how to' of art criticism. We isolate the elements of a work of art and examine each one, defining and analyzing it. There is also an examination of what *not* to consider in judging a work of art.

The third part of this book attempts to explore the questions posed in this introduction: Why has sacred art declined so drastically? How did it happen? And perhaps the most important question: What are the effects of the profane infiltrating the sacred?

In the Appendices I offer some examples of contemporary iconoclasm, excerpts of Council writings and papal encyclicals. I present these as a timeline view of how the Church has considered art; I also select various examples of artwork in which I criticize some of the characteristics essential to a work of art that are covered in this book.

Come, Holy Ghost,

fill the hearts of Thy faithful
and kindle in them the fire of Thy love.

V. Send forth Thy Spirit and they shall be created;

R. And Thou shalt renew the face of the earth.

Let us pray.

O God, who hast taught the hearts of Thy faithful by the light of
Thy Holy Spirit,
Grant us by the gift of the same Spirit
To be truly wise and have a right judgment in all things,
and evermore to rejoice in His holy comfort.

Through Christ our Lord. Amen

PART I

GOD, THE CREATOR OF HEAVEN AND EARTH

"O Sir," said I "who are the people lying

In these grim coffers, whose sharp pains disclose

Their presence to the ear by their sad sighing?"

And he: "The great heresiarchs, with all those,

Of every sect, their followers; and much more

The tombs lie laden than thou wouldst suppose."

- Dante Alighieri, The Divine Comedy: Hell

Art as a Vehicle for the Truth

Our first encounter with God as He reveals Himself is as a Creator. We learn that God created the heavens and the earth out of nothing (His idea). When He created, He saw that it was good. His will and Its manifestation were one. Creation: the physical universe, the created world, is good because God, who is All-Good, created it and said it was (reminding us that all good comes from Him).

Throughout the rest of the Old Testament, we learn the growth and development of an Idea -Redemption- which will be manifest into Reality. So, from the Bible we learn the history of Creation, Redemption and Salvation. It is not merely a string of events; it is a Perfect Work of Art. And this is a truth often overlooked: the Bible *is* a story. A story that is true. Not only is the entirety of the Bible a story, each section makes a complete story as well. The events in the Bible do not make a string, they make a story, a work of art: a work of art that is the truth. Do we really contemplate that? Might it be *necessary* to be a work of art to perfectly express the truth? I do not mean to imply that God was bound by some human rule (it must be art to be the truth) but to suggest a conformity to *God's* will. Could this possibly be a part of God's revelation? That following the creative process (working *as* or *like* an artist) in all we do is the way we can reach, or become aware of, the truth?

So, in order to understand both the significance of visual art and hence the criticism of art, we must be comfortable and familiar with thinking of God the Creator, see what is said in the Bible about art and what our Church Fathers have said and to relate this to the fact that we are made in God's image.

Let's refresh our knowledge of the importance of art from the Old Testament (coming from God rather than man). First, let's look at the First Commandment: "You shall not carve idols for yourselves." Or *"Thou shall not make graven images unto thyself."* This gives us the foundation for understanding both the significance of art as well as its purpose. Just as many misguided and superficial people have taken God's directive about marriage to mean that sex is somehow inherently bad, many also understand *this* commandment to understand that art is somehow bad, somehow forbidden. But if we come to that conclusion, we must also dismiss that we were created in God's image. God gives us directives about things that are important, not things that are not. The importance of art is known by virtue of the fact that God (besides creating the universe, a work of art) has given guidance for the creation of art. In order to instill the truth of one God, invisible and omnipresent, men were forbidden to give a form to God. Look at the words: ...not carve idols *for yourselves*. And not to make graven images *unto thyself*. God has not yet become incarnate so any image of God made by man would have to have been God made in *man's* image. We cannot create as God creates-that is, from nothing. It is only given to us to 'create' from something. If we attempt to create from nothing, we are trying to be little gods. It is blasphemy to try. That what is forbidden in this commandment. Blasphemy. We are not allowed to make God in our image. We are created in His. It is very easy to understand why God's chosen people were forbidden this activity, at this time; so easy, in fact, that one cannot help but wonder why so much has been made of it. Anyone who interprets this to mean that images should not be made is developing a theory which suits his ideology. In this environment God did not forbid art, He put limits on its creation, because His purpose is always the same: to lead us to Him. Note that man was *directed* to make an image of an angel. Angels are creatures also. Let's look at Exodus 25:17-20: we read the very specific instructions given by God for created objects to be used in worship. In describing the sanctuary for the ark to hold the commandments: *"Make two cherubim of beaten gold for the two ends of the propitiatory, fastening them so that one cherub springs direct from each end. The cherubim shall have their wings spread out above, covering the propitiatory with them; they shall be turned toward each other, but with their faces looking toward the propitiatory."* And Exodus 26:1: *"The Dwelling itself you shall make out of sheets woven of fine linen twined of violet, purple and scarlet yarn, with cherubim embroidered on them."* And in the priestly vestments (Exodus 28:33-34): *"around the hem at the bottom you shall make pomegranates, woven of violet, purple and scarlet yarn and fine linen twined, and with gold bells between them; first a gold bell, then a pomegranate, and thus alternating all around the hem of the robe."* Do these instructions sound like they come from a Being who forbids images, or a Being to whom images are of the utmost importance? If someone gave you instructions on how to bake a cake and gave great detail, which conclusion would you reach: that the person did not want you to make cakes *or* that making a cake was very important?

The Second Council of Nicaea (787) stated that *"venerable and holy images, done in color, mosaic, and all other appropriate materials, of Our Lord God and Savior Jesus Christ as well as those of Mary Immaculate, the holy Theotokos, the honorable angels and all holy and pious people are to be exposed in the holy churches of God, and on sacred vessels."*

"The Constitution of the Sacred Liturgy of the Second Vatican Council devotes a chapter (VII, paragraphs 122-129) to the dignity and purpose of sacred art in the liturgy as an assistance to worship.

In *Duodecimum Saeculum* Pope St. John Paul II writes: *"I can only invite my brothers in the episcopate to maintain firmly the practice of proposing to the faithful the veneration of sacred images in the churches"* and *"to do everything so that more works of truly ecclesial quality may be produced."* And *"Our most authentic tradition, teaches us that the language of beauty placed at the service of faith is capable of reaching people's hearts and making them know from within the One whom we dare to represent in images, Jesus Christ, Son of God made man."*

Why has the Church always recognized the significance of art?

When Pope St. John Paul II wrote about "the language of beauty" being "capable of reaching people's hearts," what does he mean? Is he talking about some emotional response that affects our 'feelings'? No, he is not. What he is referring to is the fact that as we are created in God's image, we have the capability of learning truths through art, through the creative process. Truth is always a synthesis, and as such cannot be experienced *except* through a synthetic communication, which all good art is. In other words, it is possible to learn something of Truth through art that we *cannot* learn through other means.

So, as creatures made in God's image, we have an obligation to understand the significance of art and to appreciate it as a part of the practice of worshipping, glorifying and learning from God. Understanding the importance of art, it follows that we must further see the importance of art criticism. Any offering to God, anything done for the glory of God, must be the absolute best we can do. We insult and offend God with half- hearted offerings done for ourselves.

How do we do the best we can do? The single most effective help to excellence in art is through criticism. If art criticism is either non- existent or ineffective, we can only rely on the word of the artist (his 'feelings' or 'what we like" (our 'feelings'). Any human endeavor based on emotion (how we feel) is doomed to become something trivial. Why? Because 'feelings' are not criticizable -at least not objectively criticizable. As such, they can only be *part* of following God's design for us, for it is only through obedience that we can follow God's will and obedience is an act of the will, not emotion. God's design for us is to ultimately find our way to Him. And the way (our way) to God is through the physical. Only through the physical can we get to the spiritual. Criticism is the attempt to steer our physical path, to keep it going in the right direction. Learning how to criticize art properly is part of the process of having the best art we can have to offer to God. It is an essential help to the artist. When we engage in art criticism, we have an objective model. Art criticism must be based on the truth of Trinitarian Reality. We can see that the artistic (creative) process was not man-made; it was given to man by God, it exists in every person and can be understood by every person by virtue of the fact that God created man in His image. We can see that there is a purpose to art, because it has been commanded by God; it is *not* invented by the artist *or* the viewer, even if we cannot know exactly what God's purpose is. Another necessity in our attempt to realize the importance of art (and therefore art criticism) is to think of God the Creator and God the Judge as easily as God the Father. During the Middle Ages, artists never seemed to tire of telling the great story of Creation, Redemption and Salvation. People during this time were completely at ease with the picture of God the Creator and God the Judge as well as God the Father-the idea of many facets of God (they carried a synthesis in their heads). God was often portrayed with a scale in one hand and a pair of calipers in the other. Scales even today represent justice and calipers represented the sculptor in the Middle Ages. He was just as often represented as a King, the dispenser of justice. From living in a Protestant-dominated culture, Catholics seem to have followed Protestants in thinking of God primarily as He is portrayed in the New Testament, as our Father with Jesus as our Brother. This has had a negative effect on the human mind and subsequent human behavior. As we are created in God's image, the way we define our human potential is dependent on our attempt at understanding the nature of God. If we accept a non-Catholic (heretical) vision of God, we become more and more separated from our true nature, as given by God. Certain activities that are proper to our nature-in this case the interdependent activities of making judgments and creativity (in which making judgments is a necessary component) become not only rarer and more difficult when they *are* attempted, but are also distorted and unrelated to objectivity when they are. We must understand that one cannot succumb to the temptation to simplify an idea such as Trinitarian Reality because it is a mystery. We must be comfortable with the limits of human reason. We must restudy the Nicene and the Apostle's Creeds. Catholicism requires us to stretch our minds to accept the mysteries that we cannot understand with our intellects alone. This is exactly the kind of thing that is facilitated by art.

Our Faith teaches us that God is to be understood (!) as Creator, Judge and Father. In order to be able to criticize art effectively and therefore help to raise the level of art, we must firmly fix in our minds the fact that the creative process is *not* man-made but comes from God. We must then become familiar with visualizing God in different aspects at the same time.

Finally, we must internalize the knowledge that we were made in God's image. We are all creative beings. We all carry within ourselves a deep-rooted knowledge of the creative process, although it may not be developed. That is precisely what causes us to react to a work of art in the first place. If the creative process were totally foreign to our nature, we could not care about art (or any visual image) at all. This last is an important point to understand. It changes our relationship to the artist and forms the basis for the rationality of art criticism. Until we have firmly fixed in our minds the fact that the creative process is not man-made but comes from God, that we must try to have an understanding of God based on synthesis, and until we understand that we are all meant to be creative beings (how can it be otherwise)? we cannot hope to criticize art effectively. These make up the foundation that will help to develop a proper spirit of art criticism.

Iconoclasm

Iconoclasm has been with us at least as long as recorded history. We all know the superficial definition of iconoclasm and we are all absolutely sure that as Catholics, we are not practitioners of this heresy. Of all of the prevailing ideas in our society, if there is one in which we believe there is an 'us' and a 'them' this has to be it.

Artistic creation, the making of images, is the most fundamental and simplified example of behaving like a creature created in God's image. A two-year-old child, trying to make a clay bowl, is copying God and in fact only has the impulse to try to make a clay bowl due to having been created in God's image. This creative impulse is manifest in the human child before the development of free will or reason. It is the first proof that human beings are created in God's image. It is, we might say, a direct line between us and God. Because this is so, it is easy to see that a creature whose business it is to try to separate men from God would attack the human race through any and all forms of iconoclasm. Because there *are* many forms of this evil and Satan is behind every single one. Naturally the actual destruction of images, being the most superficial, is the most obvious, just as outright murder can be seen as the most obvious disregard for the fifth commandment. But just as there are many ways besides actual murder to sin against the fifth commandment, there are many variants to the sin of iconoclasm.

If we fall short of the physical destruction of an image of Our Lady but we accept a shoddy, badly and thoughtlessly executed statue or painting of Our Lady (which we do), we are guilty of a form of iconoclasm. If we are so far from the understanding of God as Creator that we accept machine-made, mass-produced images in our churches (which we do), we are guilty of a form of iconoclasm. If we build churches without seeing the integration of imagery and architecture (which we do), we are guilty of a form of iconoclasm. If images are important because of Whom they represent and we accept low quality representations in a church (which we do), we are guilty of a form of iconoclasm. If someone destroys an image in our church and the response of the priest/bishop is "Oh, I *feel* sad, let's have a dialogue" (which it has been), we are guilty of a form of iconoclasm. We are guilty in essence because we are not approaching the creation of images with even minimal respect. In this our *minds* are not so very *essentially* different from the iconoclast with a hammer. When we accept-or create- images that are carelessly or shoddily done, we are *in no way* even *attempting* to follow God's will. He created nothing carelessly or shoddily.

"Therefore strive to be perfect as my heavenly Father is perfect."

-Matthew 5:48

What are some of the other sins of iconoclasm? What is the most creative act given to the human race to participate in? The creation of a child, the creation of a creature made in His image (the creation of an image of God). Abortion can be seen as the most extreme form of iconoclasm (the destruction of an image of God). The prevalence of the horror of pornography exists, in a large part, because of the mentality of iconoclasm (disrespect for an image of God).

It must be understood that if we have a twisted idea of *Image* every single part of our lives is negatively affected because *we ourselves are images*. If this most fundamental truth is not alive within us, we cannot hope to have a life ordered to following the will of God. Anywhere, anytime we observe less than the highest respect for an image, we see some form of the sin of iconoclasm.

(See Appendices 1 and 2)

THE EFFECT OF THE INCARNATION ON THE VISUAL ARTS

"AND THE WORD WAS MADE FLESH, and dwelt among us: and we saw His glory, the glory as of the only-begotten of the Father, full of grace and truth."

-John 1:14

"For in the mystery of the Word made flesh a new light of Your glory has shone upon the eyes of our mind, so that, as we recognize in Him God made visible, we may be caught up through Him in love of things invisible.

-The Preface of the Nativity

Trinitarian Reality and Art

We should be able to see that after the Incarnation art could never be the same. It had to change forever. And that is exactly what we do see. A hallmark of art created before the Incarnation is its uniformity. Even among high art it lacks the stamp of the *individual* artist. This was intentional to a certain extent; formulae as well as subject matter were rigidly followed. But the deeper reason (an answer to *"Why were formulae and subject matter so rigidly adhered to?"*) was that ancient man lacked the idea of the significance of the human individual that was reinforced by the Incarnation. Interestingly enough, as we become able to speak of a 'post-Christian' society, this uniformity is becoming a hallmark of contemporary art (sacred *or* secular) as well. It is what is behind the attraction to 'art' with a predictable, mass-produced look. It is because the reality of the Incarnation is either not believed, or it is being ignored.

If we review the gifts and revelations of the Incarnation, we can begin to understand why this would lead to the development of the highest and greatest body of art in human history. It is important to understand the development of art which took place after the Incarnation and continued for over 1500 years. At no other time in human history was a body of high-level art developed that was so diverse and so consistently high for so long. Art only began to deteriorate when people began to reject the complete truths contained in the Catholic faith and subsequently began to distance themselves from Trinitarian Reality.

How do the truths of the Incarnation relate to art? Man had created images from his earliest beginnings. We have had man-made images much longer than we have had history. In fact, as soon as we have man, we have art-the created image. And because the creative act is part and parcel of what it means to be human, and because the creative act is a synthesis of the physical and the non-physical, humans knew that there had to be a non-physical reality. In fact, they began making images of deities but these were based on their own life experiences. In other words, they made up a god that made personal sense. It is obvious that these could not have been sustained very well once people came into contact with other societies (who would have made up different gods for themselves). The whole process deteriorated, with men making gods at will, as many and as diverse as they wanted. The 'non-physical,' becoming something created by the physical (man) lost all meaning, deteriorating simply into different forms of superstition, which at times included satanic elements. But when God revealed Himself to man, he was invisible and transcendent. No one was able to 'see' Him. The Reality of the non-physical was reinforced to man. Eventually there came the Incarnation, when the Transcendent united to the physical. When God showed Himself to man as a physical Being, the human creative flower burst forth because the source of the human's creative impulse was shown. Since the Incarnation, it has not been possible to create high art unless the truth of the Incarnation is alive within the artist. It is revealing to note that the non-Catholic heresies since the Incarnation-which either reject the Trinity outright (Islam) (Mormonism) or minimize It (Protestantism)-have no high visual art. The few great artists of Protestantism came from Catholic roots. It would be more accurate to think of them as the last of the great Catholic artists rather than the first of the Protestant ones.

The Incarnation, Crucifixion and Resurrection teach a purpose to experience: Redemption. Evil is not transformed, but *used.* The greatest evil the world has known was *at the same time* the vehicle for the greatest Sacrifice and the greatest expression of love the world has known. An act is always itself, but it can contain more than itself. Life is not just a series of occurrences that continue until we die. It has meaning. It is our raw material, our medium, our way to God. And we can only redeem it through being creative persons. In short, through the Incarnation we were *shown* the creative process, the way to God.

" I came that they may have life, and have it to the full."

-John 10:10

LAYING THE GROUNDWORK

'Unless the Lord builds the house,

Those who build it labor in vain".

-Psalm 127

Overview of the Necessary Steps to Art Criticism

It is always thrilling when we can reach Catholic truth through purely secular means. This is what we are going to do in art criticism. There are characteristics common to all works of art, both the successful and the unsuccessful. Characteristics, or elements, that are able to be analyzed and judged. These characteristics are bound by the Trinity. They are contained in the idea, the physical work itself and the effect of the work. Of these we will concentrate on the first two. These are the things that we must consider when we criticize a work. However, first things first. Before we even begin learning how to criticize a work of art, we have to develop a mind capable of doing the job. This will be done in several steps. Our first job is to discern if the piece even *is* a work of fine art, remembering that only images of fine art belong in a church. Next, we will examine the difference between fine art and craft, and fine art and illustration. What makes work belong to the category of 'Fine Art'; what makes a work of 'Craft' or 'Illustration' and why is this distinction important? Finally, we will learn how to develop the mindset that we must bring to an artwork in order to see clearly and effectively as a critic. Remember that the purpose of *all* art must be the glorification of God. Since we can understand the importance of art from the revelation of God, we must see that man-made divisions *of kind* in the difference between secular art and sacred art are fundamentally false. It is not false to make a natural distinction of the different purposes of different art forms. But all art, whatever the purpose, must be criticized using the same criteria. All art exists for the purpose of leading people to God. (People who avoid the mention of God will say *all art exists for the purpose of leading people to truth*). The characteristics of a work of art that can be criticized apply to every work of art, whatever its purpose. There is no difference between 'secular' art or 'religious' art in this sense. From the perspective of our salvation, there is no such thing as 'secular' art. It is a man-made construct. We can criticize any form of art from the model God has given us. If this 'unreality' of secular art seems surprising, we should remember that in the entire history of art, secular art has always been a very small subset of serious art. It is only in the contemporary world, with no serious religious art, that the idea of 'secular' art looms so large.

Is It Art-or not?

The absolute, fundamental, non-negotiable criterion of all fine art-good or bad-is that the artist actually executes the work himself. There are so many ways for an artist to get away with not doing the work in this day and age that it's difficult to keep up with them, so I'll just mention a few. For example, there's the 'figurative' 'sculptor' who makes life casts on people and then puts them together. The way this is done is that the 'artist' makes a mold directly on a person's hand, for example, then the arm, and so on. After he has all the body parts he needs, he then puts them together into a pose. Then there is the sculptor who makes a small maquette, (or model) to be enlarged at a factory, the 'sculptor' who uses a 3-D printer, the painter who takes a painting or a print to a sign maker to make a stained-glass window. The ultimate is the sculptor going to a 'manufacturer' and discussing his 'idea' with the staff and they do the whole thing! Much non- objective public 'art' is done in this way. Of course, there are the mass-produced 'sculptures' and 'stained glass windows' from factories in China or wherever. None of these people/factories/assembly lines/companies is making art, good or bad, neither fine art nor fine craft nor fine illustration. Such work does not rise to the level of something to be analyzed, criticized, or looked upon in any way as fit to be in God's house. I call it non-art.

Educating Catholics about the significance of art and what constitutes a work of art is very important. However, we must keep a number of things in mind.

First of all, we must remember that before we can even discuss a work in terms of its value as a work of sacred art, that is on its transformational merit, we must first evaluate it on its purely artistic merit. Trying to convince people that they should be led to a transformation to holiness through a badly executed work or through non-art (as defined above) is very wrong and very dangerous. In so doing we are adhering to a religious viewpoint that *must* ultimately lead to trivializing the Faith-through trivializing the created world. Secondly, those raised in a society where there is no appreciation of beauty are going to prefer-at first-the bland and the not-beautiful. Raised in a materialist society that glories in 'science' and the 'cleanliness' of the idea, they are going to prefer the machine-made over the human-made, the uniform over the personal. This is surprising to some, who think that *everyone* must automatically possess a 'natural' positive response to true beauty. No, in the contemporary world the mind must be trained to appreciate the beautiful, but in the process, we must be sure we are showing people something that actually is beautiful, something that deserves to be appreciated. This is where art criticism-in other words, knowledge of the elements of a work of art, comes in. If we have no idea what the objectives governing art are, or worse still, that there even are objectives in art, how can we do anything except use art to manipulate the viewer? How can we do anything except tell the viewer how he 'should' be responding? Without knowledge, we have nothing real to teach. Without something real to teach we can only 'engineer', which is an evil substitute for education.

So, if an image has not been made by a human being, by hand, forget it. It is not art. And only real art is good enough for God's house.

The Idea of 'Art as a Teacher'

"Suddenly the Church needed to produce art and architecture on a more ambitious scale in order to accommodate and educate its new members and to reflect its new dignity and social importance. The walls of the churches were decorated with paintings or mosaics to instruct the faithful."

This was written by the editors of the *Encylopaedia Britannica* in the section on Early Christian Art. This subject has been so widely written about and is accepted by so many people that it is easy to overlook the fact that it is not only wrong, but also an extremely destructive construct. It implies that the purpose of art in the churches was to instruct and educate the people.

The claims of this or that 'purpose' of art are all misleading as well as wrong. They are misleading because they lead us into error, and wrong because they compartmentalize something which is a synthetic, integrated communication. And when we fall into an erroneous and wrong way of thinking, it skews our whole vision of that which we are examining or trying to understand. Soon we are so far from the essence of the thing that its deterioration is inevitable.

Any commandment of God is given to us for our good. As long as we obey it, it emits an infinite number of goods. If we choose to disobey a Commandment from God, there are an infinite number of evils that result. These goods or evils are both temporal and spiritual. Since we can see the immediate temporal effects, we tend to focus on them, but there are always more than our eye can see.

If people who are not allowed to be followers of Christ devise a specialized communication of asking another if he is a Christian, then we can say that the purpose of that secret communication is to find other Christians. The abstract line drawing of a fish served such a purpose in the early days of Christianity. The drawing was an invention of man, so man was allowed to state its purpose. (Anyone who does not know the beautiful symbolism in this should look it up). But man does not see as God sees, so we cannot make any sweeping assumptions about what His commandments 'mean.' When God gives a commandment-in this case the making of images-we cannot know the entirety of His 'purpose.' We follow

His command out of faith. We may be able to see good results; we may not. If we do see some good, we must always remember that this 'seeing' is a gift from God, freely given-*and partial*-not something we 'get' and certainly not something we 'deserve.' He does not owe us 'proof' that His commandments are 'worthwhile.' Certainly people-both the literate and the illiterate-can learn history such as the Bible from a work of art. They can learn history from other sources as well: the literate may learn it through reading, the illiterate through tradition. Both methods can teach history, albeit in different ways, and each method may have its proponents, but everyone, both the literate and the illiterate, receive something completely different from a work of art, something unique to the experience of art that they cannot get from any other source. A work of art is not a substitute for reading, and reading is not a substitute for art. All human beings have a deep need for all art forms: stories, poetry, music, the visual arts. The reception of the knowledge given through a work of art is essential for *all* to receive. And all viewers are equal receptors; art is not for any particular group of people, but for *all* people, and equally important for all people. All people can learn history, problem solving, cooperation, persistence, beauty, quality, the list of the 'lessons' of art could go on and on. They may also have a transforming experience which leads them to the awareness of the existence of Truth.

Note: In terms of the Church's "ambitious" architecture to "accommodate" the faithful and/or as a reflection of its importance, social or otherwise: this would be completely natural and proper, but stating it in this way reveals the total lack of understanding of the Church. We would do better to describe it thus: "Suddenly the Church realized the need to produce art and architecture on a more ambitious scale in order to accommodate more properly the presence of God Himself, as well as a signal to the world of the presence of a Divine Institution which, founded by God Himself, contains the whole Truth. The faithful would also benefit because on entering such a magnificent structure; their thoughts would be led to a different level of existence.

The Difference between Fine Art and Craft

When selecting work for the purpose of leading people to prayer, we should select from the area of fine art rather than craft (or illustration). But what's the difference? The line seems so blurred, but somehow, we always perceive the difference.

The first thing to realize is that the line drawn between 'craft' and 'fine art' is a new construct in the history of art. Although there has always been a difference between the two, the criterion for the classification has completely changed. Up until the post-Renaissance era, a young person whose parents recognized in him artistic leanings or ability would enter a studio/workshop of a master painter or sculptor. All who entered began at the same level. No one chose between a 'fine arts' program or a 'crafts' program. All students began learning the same things; so that in a painter's workshop they would all learn to grind colors, mix the colors, mix gesso, prepare the wood panel, and so on. In a sculptor's workshop they would learn to mix clay, build armatures, mix plaster, cast, block out stone, etc. As the technical repertoire of the student grew, he would constantly add on to his knowledge. He would continue in this way, adding onto his knowledge, until he reached his potential, that is, the point beyond which he could not progress. At that level he would find his area of work. One might not progress beyond the preparation stage; he might find work as an artist's assistant. Someone else might excel at painting backgrounds, which would be his job, and so on. In this way the student would naturally work according to his abilities and therefore discover his true creative potential. He understood his limits, which freed him to excel at what he did best.

The summit of the apprentice's training was always the human figure. Excellence in the human figure was recognized as the highest level of artistic activity. This remained true until the introduction of 'abstraction' in the late nineteenth and early twentieth centuries.

Was this earlier attitude toward the figure an arbitrary judgment? No, it was not. It was based on basically three things:

1. Mastering the human figure is a long and arduous task. It is not merely a question of observation and drawing practice; it requires the study of anatomy. This takes not only dedication but also tenacity, intellectual ability, persistence, and attention to detail on a level that most people become impatient with, and humility. The artist must be willing to spend countless hours working on something which is not art, to memorize hundreds of facts *and* to try to correlate his intellectual knowledge with the ability to paint or sculpt it-a monumental task.

2. The artist knows that his job is never done. On a certain

level he must retain the mind of a student all his life, constantly studying and practicing. You can easily see that not everyone with artistic ability has the temperament or the desire to study anatomy and therefore to master the figure.

3. The theological idea that was accepted up until the late nineteenth century was that the human being is the summit of God's terrestrial creation. The awareness of this is what drove (and drives) an artist to go through the process of learning anatomy. It also accounts the respect that was given to the figurative artist, both by other artists as well as non-artists.

What all of this meant was that when someone was looking for a painter or a sculptor to make a religious work, he naturally chose an artist who knew the figure; this meant that (without using the terminology) he was choosing a fine artist. Whereas if he were looking for an artist to make something that did not include the figure (again, without using the word) he could employ a craftsman, i.e., someone who had not spent the time learning anatomy. Obviously, he would not have to pay as much, which was proper. So, this is one way of describing the difference between fine art and craft: the 'fine artist' has mastered-or is in the process of mastering-the figure; the 'craftsperson' is focused on other things. His focus is not the figure; to him it is just another subject, not something worth a lifetime of study. This goes a long way in terms of understanding the decline of religious art: too many people are trying to make figurative works without this love and dedication to the study of the anatomy of the human figure. The craftsperson may make beautiful objects for use in the liturgy, which is essential. But the anatomy of the figure is simply not his primary concern. Another possibility is that the artist in question is neither a craftsperson nor a fine artist, but an illustrator.

The Difference between Illustration and Fine Art

This is another area in which two things are sometimes, and erroneously, seen as basically the same thing. They are not. The line is blurrier than in the difference between fine art and craft, but it is real and definite nonetheless. One difference is the artist's focus and what he sees as the end (purpose) of the work. The illustrator, usually looking to have the work printed, i.e., mass produced, is focusing on how the work *looks*. He asks "what does it look like?" The fine artist asks "Am I reaching the essence of this thing?"

Another difference is that the illustrator expresses himself without the need for a personal relationship with the viewer. A reproduction of an illustration loses none of its meaning; the work of fine art can never be fully appreciated unless the viewer is looking at the actual original work. Another difference is that the illustrator doesn't mind working from other work or photographs; he is concerned more with symbols of things. The fine artist always works from life, he always feels a need to digest and express something about nature, the physical world; he is more concerned with the reality of things. For example, an illustrator may set up a model in the pose he needs, but then may photograph the model and work from the photograph and this is fine with him. The fine artist feels a need to work from the model directly.

Because the illustrator is concerned with the appearance of a thing, many people looking for a religious artist and seeing that the illustrator's work looks 'realistic', or representational, will hire an illustrator to complete a work that should be done by a fine artist. This is understandable since many self-identified 'fine artists' equate 'fine art' to mean sloppy, slipshod and 'abstract' in some way. Most 'fine' artists have not taken the time and effort to learn anatomy and attempt to cover their ignorance with some 'philosophy.' However, the illustrator has not taken the time to learn anatomy either, except perhaps on the superficial level of 'what does it look like.' The problem is that the illustrator cannot just suddenly put on a fine artist's cap. They are different people with a completely different focus. So, if the illustrator is commissioned to do what should be a work of fine art, such as a painting or a sculpture for the inside of a church, it will not do what it is supposed to do; it *cannot* do the job of sacred fine art.

There is no shortcut. The priest looking for a religious figurative image for the inside of a church must take the time to find a fine artist that knows anatomy. Resist the temptation to be impressed by a 'realistic' work. We will discuss the difference between realistic and representational in Part II.

Quite possibly one of the most important difference between fine art and craft, or fine art and illustration, is that fine art makes demands on the viewer that neither craft nor illustration make. Both craft and illustration provide an immediate response in the viewer; the viewer is able to respond to what he sees immediately; he doesn't need to reflect. Fine art requires the viewer to bring something to the table, so to speak. It is more of an invitation than a directive. This is why fine art can be looked at over a long time and can continue to give. An illustration or a work of craft gives all it can in the first viewing. One may like the work and look at it repeatedly, but what it gives has been given; any later appreciation comes from *inside* the viewer-for example, as he contemplates the 'meaning' the work has for *him*-not from *outside* the viewer, that is, from the work itself. It is a *subjective, emotional* (smaller) experience rather than an *objective, intellectual* (bigger) one. We have become so accustomed to expecting a 'wow' quality in visual images (a subjective experience), that many dismiss a work when it is not present. But this 'wow' quality may not be there in a work of fine art; it is not a requirement for fine art. Think of it as a first impression when we meet a new person. If we wish to get to know the person and to learn what that person has to give, we must be prepared to take the time which is necessary.

Finally, a good way to distinguish the difference between illustration and fine art is this: the illustrator gives facts. Facts are important and are a part of the truth, but the truth is not *a part* of the facts. Truth encompasses facts; facts do not encompass truth. The fine artist (no matter if he fails) is looking for the essential truth about a thing. This is one reason why people like illustrations; looking at them requires less of an effort and the response is always the same and therefore predictable. Think of a child reading a picture book: one reason he loves the pictures is because of the sense of familiarity, he can anticipate his response. The very predictability is what the child loves. Unfortunately, many people mistake predictability for proof that something is true. This response of a child should not be encouraged in the mature believer. More *should* be required of Catholics as they develop and mature.

(See Appendices 4, 5, 6)

One can see that in the Medieval world the difference among types of artists was dependent on *objectivity*; in the post Renaissance world the difference began to depend more and more on the *self-identification* of the artist *(subjectivity),* where unfortunately it rests today.

Note: Please be aware that I am not making any judgment concerning a work of illustration compared to a work of fine art. An illustration may be of the highest quality; a work of fine art may be of the lowest. I am merely pointing out the differences in the methodology and approach of each different type of artist, and that it is the working method of the illustrator that makes his work inappropriate for the inside of a Catholic church.

How to Prepare Yourself to Look at a Work of Art

Our contemporary minds are filled with much that is a hindrance to and stands in the way of looking at art. In the great painter Giotto's time, about 800 years ago, the peasants around him were not educated in our sense of the word. Most could neither read nor write. They were materially poor by our standards, did physical rather than intellectual work. And yet, stories have come from that time that describe the love and appreciation they had for Giotto's work. Giotto painted many very large paintings but there was never a problem about transport; the villagers would fight for the honor of carrying the paintings from studio to church. We know that Giotto painted in a way that was completely new. What gave the 'uneducated' peasants their vision? The work was completely different from what they were accustomed to. But no one had to tell them it was good; they recognized the excellence. How?

The reason is very simple. It is because they dealt with reality and we do not. Sounds simple, but what exactly does it mean?

What happened to the human mind when we decided to look inward rather than outward for the authority of truth, which is what happened at the Protestant revolt? Immediately we separated ourselves from Reality; we insulated ourselves from Objectivity.

Subject, not Object, became for us the only, or at least, the main reality. Areas of human activity such as art that touch us holistically, that is both objectively and subjectively are not exempt from objective guidelines. We behave as if they are only because we first divorced the intellect from the emotions (the objective from the subjective), and then re-introduced it (the intellect) as a human accoutrement *to* the emotions. We must understand that the human being is a unit, that the free will comes from God to guide our intellect. The emotions, because they can be influenced by most anything: the weather, our health, others' approval or disapproval of us, etc. should be met with a degree of skepticism. If the emotion we feel conforms to the will and the intellect, we can have a powerful, sometimes transformational experience. Which is exactly what a serious work of fine art does; it causes a transformation in us. When we give too much credence to the subjective, we *must* compartmentalize our mind, because the subjective (emotion) cannot encompass the objective (will and intellect). The smaller can never encompass the larger. The result is that we actually begin to block ourselves off from transformational experiences. And this upside-down compartmentalizing (from emotion to intellect to will) means we will not be effective critics of art-or anything else for that matter.

The peasant viewer in the Middle Ages had something we do not: a receptive mind. It was receptive-the first stage in knowledge-because he *knew* that Truth was objective to him. His mind was much more unified with his emotions because the objective really can encompass the subjective. This made him more open to what he saw and felt. He trusted his response more because his response was more trustworthy. To say he measured what he saw against what he knew to be true implies probably even more of a separation than was there. His *mind* held the truth that his emotional response supported. His response was more integrated and complete, more of a *total* response. As such, he was more in tune with the *essence* of a thing rather than its *accidents*. Which is why he could see the superiority in one image of Our Lord over another, even if he could not explain it. He *recognized* it. *He knew the truth when he saw it.*

This quality of receptivity is necessary if we are to look without preconceptions: to deal with reality. We cannot judge a work of art effectively if, for example, we are responding to our 'ideas,' by which we mean 'feelings' (subjectivity, emotion), about the work.

Our modern minds are fragmented and disjointed, a process that began with the Fall and has continued since then to bring us to the point at which we are now-the point at which we have lost the ability to really *look* at something and be able to pass an 'instinctive' judgment.

So, how do we fix this? First of all, by remembering that God constructed our minds to be unified. As such, we must first direct our will in the direction of unity. Then we must use our intellect to seek out practices that help us to develop a unified mind. Here are some suggestions: 1) keep at least one holy hour per week in front of the Blessed Sacrament; 2) learn to draw. Anyone can learn to draw from nature. I have listed a book to assist you in the *suggested reading list at* the end of this book. Please do not say that you can't draw or that you have no artistic talent. *Any* person can learn to draw. *Anyone. Everyone* has enough artistic talent and intelligence to learn to draw (although you may not believe it looking at most contemporary artwork). It should be considered a basic skill, like reading and writing; 3) learn to play a musical instrument. Same as drawing; 4) read poetry and/or listen to good music. Notice that the kinds of activities that will help to develop a more unified mind are creative ones. The practice of creativity gives you understanding of the creative process, which will make you a better critic.

<u>**Part II**</u>

THE ELEMENTS OF A WORK OF ART

"Wherefore by their fruits you shall know them. Not everyone who says to me 'Lord, Lord' will enter the kingdom of Heaven, but only the one who does the will of My Father in Heaven."   *-Mt 7:21*

"I do not want you to be unaware, brothers, that our ancestors were all under the cloud and all passed through the sea, and all of them were baptized into Moses, in the cloud and in the sea. All ate the same spiritual food, and all drank the same spiritual drink, for they drank from a spiritual rock that followed them, and the rock was the Christ.

    Yet with most of them God was not well pleased."

        -The first letter of St. Paul to the Corinthians

"The supreme misfortune is when theory outstrips performance."

        -Leonardo da Vinci

Overview of the Elements of a Work of Art

In this section we will proceed to defining the elements of a work and learning how to analyze them. The elements in the work itself that we will consider are: 1) the **Integration** or **Composition** 2) the **Idea;** 3) the **Technical Expertise** of the artist, with a section on **Anatomy Abstraction;** 4) the **Development of the Work;** and 5) the **Conclusion of the Work.** The two most important of these elements are the *Idea* and the *Composition.* On these the work depends. If either of these is deemed unsuccessful, there is no need to criticize further because the work is simply bad. Only if both the idea of the work and its composition are sound do we proceed to the remaining elements., but all of these are subordinate to both the Idea and the Composition. I have put the Composition first simply because it is the first thing that meets our eyes. Lastly, 6) we will look at the concepts of **Sincerity, Fashion, Style** and their misapplication for art criticism, and finally the disastrous effects on art of **Art History**. In the Appendices, I analyze successful and unsuccessful examples of the five characteristics of a work of art.

1) <u>The Integration / Composition</u>

When we look at a work in terms of its *Integration*, we are referring to the *Composition* of work and one way to understand how to criticize this element is to look at the universe that God created. Everything is interrelated and fits together, with every object (in its essence) being developed to its fullest extent. The quality of the composition is of the utmost importance because it-along with the *Idea*-is the most fundamental aspect of an artwork. If the composition is not good, the work cannot be good. This is because the composition is our gateway into the piece. It is the first thing we see.

One way to know if the composition of a work is good is to observe our immediate reaction to it. If the composition is whole, we take pleasure in the mere sight of the work. We do not rush to think of what it is, that is *"What is it supposed to be about"*? Something within us is *satisfied*, even if we cannot see the subject matter. Also, a complete composition is like an umbrella over the whole; we see the big, which leads us into smaller parts. We are also able to see how the smaller sections fit into the larger. A perfect example of beautiful composition and is an illustration of this is to look at the rose windows in Chartres Cathedral. The reason that good composition is an essential characteristic of good art is because it follows the creative process. The creative process consists of beginning with a limit (in this case the overall design of the windows), and working your way inward, making something new at every stage, always starting with a new limit, and again going inward. The creative process is followed.

One way of following good composition is to utilize the golden section, or the golden ratio. This is a system of proportion that exists in many places in nature. It exists when a line is divided into two (uneven) parts, and the longer part (a) divided by the smaller part (b) is equal to the sum of (a) + (b) divided by (a), which both equal 1.618 (!). It is the way rose petals and conch shells grow, as well as applying to the proportions of the human body. It has been used since antiquity. It is part of created reality and is a beautiful way of organizing composition, but, if I dare say it, it is not quite complete.

We know that everything changed at the Incarnation. Things that were true before the Incarnation continued to be so, but things were fulfilled, and the concept of composition is one of them. *Seeming* contradictions began to be fitted together. This fitting together of *seeming* opposites or contradictions, became one of the elements of good composition that cannot be ignored. Two key words that seem to be contradictory when criticizing composition are: **integrated** and **diverse**. Integration does *not* mean treating different elements in the same way. Integrity married to diversity is one of the Truths of the universe that God created which we learned with the Incarnation. For example, if the artist either paints or sculpts the hair in exactly the same way as the drapery so that they fit together, this is not good composition, *even if it follows the Golden Ratio.* This is because it is not complete composition at all. Good composition means attempting to treat all elements according to their proper nature which is different, but finding a way to make it into an integrated whole. An excellent example of this principle of composition would be the paintings of Rembrandt. Remember that good art is always a synthesis. In other words, we must look for the twin truths of diversity developed to a high degree, and integration developed to a high degree. When trying to tell the truth, nothing essential can be eliminated. Looking at the composition, we cannot allow ourselves to be focused on the subject matter; we must remain independent. It is very easy to allow ourselves to be influenced by what the painting or sculpture is about, our feelings or opinions about what it is about. This, however, would not be dealing with reality; it would be dealing instead with ourselves rather than the work.

When we look at a work of art with the objective of criticizing its composition, we consider the following:

- Does the overall beauty of the work strike us immediately? Not the beauty of the superficial (perfect people or a lovely scene-remember we are trying to remain independent of the subject) but the sense of satisfaction that comes from an integrated statement. Or do we have to *immediately* focus on the subject matter, on what it *is*.(bad) Always think in terms of going from the general to the specific. If we see a toddler trying to walk, we respond to the entirety of the child first before we see the color of his eyes or even the features of his face. (good)

- Does everything fit together? Does every part fit with every other part, *yet remain distinct*? For example, is the skin on a figure treated differently than the bark of a tree or a piece of clothing? (good)

- Is there anything in the work that jars us, that does not contribute to the feeling of wholeness? (bad)

- Are our first thoughts things like: "That leg is just too long" or "What's that supposed to be?" And do these things prevent us from concentrating on the meaning of the piece? (bad)

- Do we feel-or are we made to feel-that we need a special education in order to appreciate the work? (bad) Is the composition made up of sequential, disjointed pieces or does it seem to create an integrated whole? (disjointed-bad, integrated-good)

- Are the spaces between objects beautiful and do these relate to the 'spaces' considered as the objects? (empty space- bad) *Everything* must be considered.

- Do we get the sense that the piece is *completely* made up of positive decisions or that maybe just the figures are focused on and the rest is just 'background' or empty? (positive decisions-good)

- Do our eyes naturally desire to look at the whole piece or do we tend to dwell on one section and want to ignore the rest? Do our eyes want to skip sections of the piece? Do we want to keep looking at it? (skip sections-bad)

- Is it *all* beautiful? (good) Are there any boring parts? For example, if there is a large section of drapery is it just a large empty form or is it alive? (boring and empty-bad)
- Is there a sense of balance? Balance and symmetry are two classical means of achieving good composition. (See Appendices 7, 8, 9, 10, 11, 12, 13)

2) <u>The Idea</u>

Just as the will in a person is the core, and must be oriented correctly, so the idea in the artist must be sound. Everything rests on the idea. It is the other fundamental characteristic in a work of art. The *Idea* and the *Composition* are the twin essences: if either one is bad, go no farther. The work should be disregarded.

So, what is this 'idea'? When we look at the idea of a work of art, we must be aware that this *idea* of a piece exists on several levels, or layers, from the most superficial to the deepest. Just remember: if a work fails on the level of the *Idea,* forget it. Don't bother to criticize it further. It doesn't matter if the work is executed with technical perfection. It doesn't matter how 'realistic' it is. If the idea is not correct/good, the work is useless. The *Idea* is the justification for the existence of the work. So how do we criticize something which is non-material? By remembering that the physical and the non-physical worlds make up a unit, and as such that the non-physical will always find some expression into the physical. Since the ***idea*** of a work is so complex, we will break it down into sections, which will include:

- ***Subject Matter (layer one)***
- ***Interpretation of the Story (layer two)***
- ***Choice of Size (layer three***
- ***Use of Symbolism (layer three)***
- ***The Purpose of the Work (layer three)***
- ***Choice of Medium (layer three)***
- ***Is it God's Will vs. Does it work (layer four)***

- ***Subject Matter***

First of all, there is the ***subject matter***. This is the most superficial layer of the idea. If the artist is using Biblical or religious themes, it is assumed that the idea is sound, and on this most superficial level of subject matter this is *probably* true. When we criticize the idea of a piece on the level of subject matter, we must ask some questions. The most fundamental is: What is the story being told and is it being told accurately?

Artists sometimes, in their desire for originality and individuality, change the actual history a bit, or sometimes more than a bit. It will be because the artist has tried to inject 'individuality' at the wrong place in the creative process. Artists also, like everyone else, sometimes simply follow the fashion of the moment. And yes, there are fashions in art. This is a grave error and twists and pollutes the idea. The thrust of the artist's idea becomes egoistic, his idea is to express the pride he feels in himself, rather than the true story. The critic has a responsibility to steer the artist to represent the true story. A way to know if this most basic element is successful is to ask yourself if someone, without knowing what the image is *supposed* to represent, would be able to know at least the physical facts by just looking at the work. For example, if you are looking at a painting which represents the Ascension of Our Lord, someone who knows nothing of the history may not learn it by looking at the painting. But the person should be able to tell that a very special man is rising up toward the sky, that there are a certain number of people present and get a sense of the glory and wonder of the event. When he reads the Biblical account, he will be able to see that the image is an illustration of what he has read. If this is not completely clear, if the man in the painting does not look holy or the gloriousness is not apparent, or if the figure is abstracted and could be a creature from outer space and ceases to represent a human being (we must remember that God became *man*), if the factual history is changed in any way, that is the first level of criticism. So, the critic must ask firstly if the proper history is being told, and if not, must steer the artist back to the facts.

• *Interpretation of the Story*

The next level of the *Idea* is the **Interpretation of the Story**. Here is where knowledge of the meaning of the event is either apparent or not. It is seeing the subject matter in a deeper sense. An example of this would be in a representation of the Holy Family. At the time of this writing there is a fashion among artists to portray the Virgin Mary, Saint Joseph and Our Lord and Savior as a newborn as though they were the suburban family across the street, or the poverty-stricken family in the housing project. In the first what we usually see are two doting parents gushing over their newborn child, in the second a despairing family group. Period. These representations are a contraction of the meaning of the event. Although it may pass the first criteria of criticism since there is a father, mother and baby shown, it fails miserably against this second level of *idea*. The true meaning of the story (that it represents God Himself and a sinless woman) is not examined; the figures are only thought of on the natural level and the supernatural is ignored. Whatever the reason-either the artist believes that he can improve upon the true story, or he doesn't really believe the true story (that is, it is not living within him), or he thinks he can explain the 'true' meaning of the story, it doesn't matter. You are still left with an inferior work of art, because the work fails on the *Idea*.

(See Appendices 14, 15, 16,17)

- ### *Choice of Size*

A third element of the *Idea* is the ***Choice of the Size*** of the work. Some points outside of the artist to consider: where the piece will be placed, how it will be placed, the purpose of work. But whatever space, the artist should always make the piece as large as possible. It should fill the space. We must consider the choice of size very carefully when developing the idea. Should an image (painting or sculpture) of Our Lord or Our Lady be life-sized, over life- sized, or smaller? A general rule is that whenever possible it should be over life-sized. If the circumstance demands that it be smaller than life-sized, the image should be placed so that we are looking *up* at the image as much as possible. We should try never to look *down* on an image of Our Lord (except of course Our Lord as a Baby in a manger). If the work is a painting or a relief, the shape of the frame (outer limits) of the work become part of the idea and as such become open to criticism. There must be consideration of how we situate a painting or sculpture which represents a sacred subject. In other words, the size, shape and placement of a piece are integral parts of the idea being expressed. Remember that the person commissioning the work is the artist's guide and as such has a responsibility to ensure that the whole idea of the work is sound. Also, (as the mind is receptive) be aware that if the idea of the artist is different from yours, and it is not a matter of dogma, listen to him but require him to justify himself. You may decide to follow his idea, but this would probably be only in a situation where you already know the artist's work and trust his decisions. You are not trying to tell the artist how to work; rather you are aware of and responding to the responsibility you both have. You tell the artist *what* to do; he uses his own creativity in *how* he does it. The 'what' and the 'how' should flow, one from the other. You and the artist should have the same goals. If you don't, rethink your choice of artist.

• *Use of Symbolism*

Symbolism plays a part in much religious work as well as playing an extremely major role in the idea in icons. Many of the greatest artworks utilize symbolism. Actually, it is difficult to keep it out of religious work. But the use of symbolism is a great artistic challenge. It is a very difficult thing to keep alive. For example, the symbolism of contemporary icons has the taint of academic formulae. Most icons look as though the artist thinks the work exists to serve the symbol and this is exactly the challenge in using symbolism. Symbolism should always be secondary (or tertiary) in a work of art. It can never be sighted as *the* reason for value in any work. It enriches the work; the value of the work does not depend on the symbolism.

> *"The Sabbath was made for man, not man for the Sabbath."*
>
> *-MK 2:27*

• *The Purpose of the Work*

When placing artwork inside of a church, keep in mind its **Purpose.** The purpose is not to entertain or wow the people. The ultimate purpose is to lead them to prayer and a meditative state. Images also set the stage for the Holy Sacrifice of the Mass, and will have a positive or a negative effect (never neutral) on the priest celebrating Mass. The priest may also have a more specific purpose for a particular work. Always remember that how appropriately a work meets its purpose is another thing that lies within the job of the critic.

• *Choice of Medium*

The next part of the idea to consider is the **Medium** or the **Material.** There is a relationship between the material used and the success of the execution of the idea. Artists use their hands to manipulate materials and the choice of material can never be arbitrary. Remember that the actual work is the manifestation of an idea and that the choice of medium, being a vehicle for the idea's expression, is an integral part of the idea.

One of the characteristics of contemporary society is the over emphasis on the importance of words (the written word) as *the* medium for expression. We accept the idea that words are the ultimate test for the validity of an idea. We don't see words as *a* medium of expression; we see words as *the* medium for expression. This is a fruit of the Protestant idea of 'sola scriptura.' We do not understand that words are only one of a variety of media to express an idea. Of course we do not realize that we have accepted this; it only comes to light in our undervaluing of the visual arts and music, for example. As it happens, visual artists express ideas when engaged in making a work of art in a medium other than words. They may use paint (color), line, form, clay, stone, glass or mosaic. These materials are their words. Just as when we speak or write we must be careful to say things in the right way, using the correct words and grammar, so must the artist use the correct medium when he is expressing his idea. Here are some questions to use as a guideline for criticism of the medium used:

- Has the artist used the correct (best) medium for the expression of his idea? When looking at a work, picture that same work in another medium. Does the work gain or lose in merit with the change? If it gains, it has been done in the wrong medium. Unfortunately, artists sometimes force all of their visions into one medium because most artists select a medium based on what they have been trained in. Ask him if he can work in other media.

- Is the artist trying to express an idea through sculpture that would be better represented in painting? Or vice-versa? Is the artist working in stone when bronze would be more suitable? Or vice-versa? Has he perfected his manipulation of the medium? The same subject can be expressed in different media, but the artist must connect not just the subject matter but the deeper level of the idea to his choice of medium. Can he see the different artistic considerations between a painting of the crucifixion and a sculpture of one?

- Each medium has its own set of limits. Has the artist understood and respected that?

This is another reason why the work must be completely done by the artist himself. The artist who does not do the work himself is not sensitive to the relationship between the idea and the medium. And remember that in order to adhere to the goal of religious art; we should stick to traditional media: egg tempera, oil or encaustic for paintings; stone, bronze or wood for sculpture; mosaic. The idea of creating the religious or the sacred or any high-level work of fine art and the idea of innovation are ideas which conflict; they are opposing ideas which cannot be reconciled. You cannot serve two gods at once. The time and place for the artist to be 'original' is in how he interprets the idea within the limits given. Two of the limits for him are: 1-the factual history; and 2-the proper medium. Creativity is going deeper and deeper within limits, not tearing down the limits. Anyone can do that.

(See Appendices 18, 19)

- ### *Summary of the Idea: Is it God's Will? Vs. Does it work?*

What is the fundamental springboard of the idea? The true purpose of the work? As pointed out by the art historian Sir Kenneth Clarke, something in man changed at the Renaissance. And what changed was that the question asked by Medieval man was *"Is it God's will?"* The question asked by Renaissance man was *"Does it work?"* That's the question we are still asking. We see our actions totally in terms of their 'result' or 'success,' in utilitarian terms. And since man does not see as God sees, this must always mean 'earthly' success. For example, the artist paints a painting or sculpts a sculpture. In his mind: *"What do I want to 'say' in this work?" "How do I want the viewer to 'feel' when he looks at this work?" "How can I 'wow' the viewer best?"* He is totally focused on whether or not 'it works.' The question in his mind is *"Does it work?"* He is *not* working for the glory of God. He is really working for his own glory. God comes in second. First, he looks at the values of the world, then he (re)acts, to those values. Until the artist changes his focus, until he tries to please God in his work, first, unequivocally first, rather than man, all of his work will be wanting. And don't allow yourself to accept the assertion that anyone can do both. No one can. We can only do one or the other. And we have proof. Listen to an interview with an artist about his work. What you hear is *"I was trying to express this", "I was trying to express that", "I was trying to say... (and of course I succeeded")*. Man and God are not equals. Our job is to glorify God. In so doing we are-or should be-pleasing man. If we are not, let the man be.

3) <u>The Technical Expertise of the Artist</u>

Technical expertise is another part of the value of a work of art. This may seem obvious, but it is true for perhaps an unexpected reason. Technical expertise is pleasurable to see, but it can be seen in furniture making as easily as in a work of fine art. It is not peculiar to fine art; we don't particularly need fine art to see or appreciate technical expertise. It is important because it frees the artist. It does not free the artist *from* the creative struggle; it frees him *to be involved* in the creative struggle. How do we know when an artist does not possess technical mastery? Here again there are objective things to observe.

First of all, we must define technical expertise. It covers knowledge of the medium-in either the use of the material, knowledge of form in sculpture or the use of color in painting-and knowledge of anatomy and drawing.

The artist must be in control of his medium. The lack of this control can be seen in a work of art that never leaves the first level, that of illustration of an event. In sculpture it is seen in works which have the stamp of being manufactured. In either painting or sculpture the underlying feeling is an over-finished, assembly-line, amateurish look. This is because the artist relies on finishing techniques that disguise his lack of knowledge and control of the medium and yet give a 'professional' look. In a bronze (or other metal) sculpture it means that the artist had to give control of the casting or other part of the sculpture-making process to a foundry; if stone or wood it means that the artist does not know how to carve and gave control to a factory. In painting the lack of technical expertise can most easily be seen in the misuse of color. Are the colors too obvious? What I mean by this is: when an artist cannot mix colors properly, he may resort to using the color straight out of the tube. They lack depth, subtlety and individuality. The painter thinks through color. If he uses colors straight out of the tube, you could say that he is not thinking deeply. Another problem with color would be the colors looking muddy rather than luminous. Mixing a luminous grey or other neutral color is difficult and requires much practice and knowledge. Colors must be luminous and deep. They should invite the viewer to inward meditation, not startle or shock him. The work should not look like a painted sign. Another gimmick of the painter involves *how* he applies color. He may try to use brush strokes that try to shock or jolt the viewer; he may use something other than a brush to apply color. In any medium it can be seen in a lack of knowledge of anatomy. We will discuss anatomy in further detail below. A good rule of thumb is that you should never be aware of the technique. Think of the Sistine Chapel's ceiling. Much has been written about Michelangelo's technical expertise, and he certainly was a master technician, but the average viewer just sees powerful painting and is unaware of any 'technique.' It should almost look easy.

There is however one thing about technical expertise that is essential to keep in mind. As important as it is, that is, a work of art cannot be good without it, remember that it is not something which can stand alone. In other words, it must be included in a successful work of fine art but does not in itself make a work great. It is so especially important when looking at technical expertise because this is something that an artist may develop when he has serious weaknesses in the other areas. For example, he may be working in the wrong medium for his idea. That would mean that his idea is badly executed, which is much more important than the 'expertise' he shows. He may have other parts of his idea that are badly formed, any of which makes the work useless, no matter how wonderful the technical mastery. Because technical expertise is always admired, many artists think that if they can develop this to an impressive degree, then they will be great artists. They may become great craftsmen but they will never be great artists. (See Appendices 20, 21)

❖ Anatomy and Abstraction

Anatomy

If an artist is creating figures, which must be the case in religious work, does the artist know anatomy? Remember, this is the dividing line between fine art and craft or illustration, and you should be looking for a fine artist. To be effectively critical in this area, the critic must be strict. We have come to believe that we must accept either the vague and imprecise *'abstract'* work of the self-proclaimed 'fine artist' *or* the superficially *'realistic'* work of the illustrator or craftsperson. This either/or is not true and the critic commissioning the work must exert his right to critical input of the work (and be ready for the artist to balk).

Figurative work done by an artist who does not know anatomy has several problems. One is an unmistakable air of amateurism. The artist can never be free to develop the idea when he is constantly on the level of worrying about how to paint or sculpt an arm or a hand. Such work can never get beyond the superficial and so can never lead the viewer to real prayer. The artist will probably resort to distractions to fool the viewer, the easiest of which is 'abstraction' in one form or another. Another problem with work in which the artist does not know anatomy is that the viewer is distracted by *what does the work look like* or *which period in history can I compare it to.*

There is another aspect to the idea of knowledge of anatomy which underlines its importance. We must keep in mind that God has chosen to have a special relationship with *man*. Man, in his complete nature: bones, muscles, skin, etc. as well as his mind and spirit. God created *man* in His image. God became *man*. To arbitrarily abstract the physical nature of man when creating a work of religious art is a sacrilege.

The critic of anatomy must look at works of art that have been done anatomically correctly, must look at human beings carefully, and must place equal emphasis on both an idea and its execution. Any serious critic should look carefully at a good art anatomy book. *Above all, the patron, and therefore the critic, should not ask the artist if he has studied or if he knows anatomy.* There are two kinds of figurative artists: those that think they know anatomy and those who do not think anatomy is important. The second group should be disregarded, and from the first the vast majority is mistaken. This is not entirely the fault of the artist; others must share the blame. Art schools tell students that if they take a few life-drawing classes and 'observe,' that's all there is to anatomy. Many art schools do not even offer this much. Priests seem perfectly happy to readily accept 'realism' in lieu of anatomical correctness. Anatomical knowledge should be self-evident in a work. If it is not, one may assume that the artist does not have it.

Anatomy is a difficult subject that takes years of study, sometimes life-long study. Why should religious artists undertake such an endeavor when they have learned from both Puritanical teachers *and* their patrons that it is not really important anyway? It's both tempting and easy to believe that something which is difficult doesn't really matter. None of the above covers *anatomical abstraction,* which we will discuss next.

Abstraction

There are two different kinds of abstraction. One kind is perfectly legitimate and one kind should be completely rejected in any work of art, sacred or not. The *conscious choice* to focus on abstraction as an essence of a work, to decide to work 'abstractly' reveals a deep-rooted sickness of the soul in the artist. Any artist that does not look to nature as being the essential limit and medium through which his ideas are expressed thinks of himself as a god. He does not understand his position in the universe; he has no sense of proportion and his work is a sacrilege. He is inserting his 'individuality' in the wrong place at the wrong time. He does not grasp the most elemental and fundamental characteristic of the process of human creation-which is that, unlike God, man cannot create from nothing. If an artist is totally focused on expressing his 'idea' or his 'feelings' he is from the outset minimizing the objective, physical world. How can such an artist be saying anything true about the universe when he minimizes creation and the physical? It is a serious misfortune that this ideology is not only encouraged but actually taught in art schools. But it becomes an outrage when embraced by the Catholic Church. Abstraction, and its younger siblings, Non-objectivity and

Conceptualism, make up the modernist art academic.

The main uses of artistic abstraction are to distract the viewer or to hide ignorance. The artist mistakenly believes that abstraction gives his work an air of mystery, which he equates with depth of thought. The underlying philosophy of abstract or non-objective art is *always* based on the avoidance or the circumvention of nature, of the physical. Simply put, the figurative artist must love the human body. Any artist trying to raise his work to the level of telling the truth and finds no joy in learning how to perfect the representation of God's highest creation is doomed to failure.

However, all this is not to say that there is no place for abstraction *as such* in figurative art. The question to ask is *"What is the nature of the abstraction?"* If we look at a work in which the artist seems to have decided to minimize the importance of anatomy, then that is probably just what he has done. And if so, it is a legitimate use of abstraction. How do we know? There are some clues. First, if we look at the 'abstracted' or 'incorrect' figures, we may see upon closer inspection that they are not so much abstract or incorrect as un-proportional or that certain things are emphasized. That is, the head or a hand is done correctly but it may be too large or too small. Or, we may see that they are abstract but completely proportional. Or, we will see other parts of the work which prove the artist's love of the physical. For example, the artist may abstract in order to make a better, more complete composition. But *something* is correct. Second, looking closely at the figure, we do not see any indecision or sloppiness. It is not unfinished or slipshod. We do not get the impression that something was overlooked. There is no feeling of avoiding the physical, of trying to give us the 'idea' of a human at the expense of the reality. Above all, we accept it. We accept the artist's leadership. Remember that the artist is leading us, which means that his decision to minimize or maximize anatomy may be a tool to lead us to his conclusion. What is he leading u s to? Well, when we criticize the work, it is our responsibility to ask. If we understand that he is leading us to an understanding of the superiority or the importance of the supernatural over the physical, then his use of abstraction may be perfectly legitimate. It is a question of using nature to lead us to the supernatural. Such an artist does not avoid nature or pass her by; he goes through her. The important thing to remember always is that it is the patron's duty and responsibility to ask if something is not obvious to him. If the artist takes offense, this would be a signal that he does not understand the significance of religious art or the purpose of art in general. Don't work with him.

Here we can learn much from work that does not meet the above stated requirements for anatomical correctness and yet reaches the level of not only high art but also sacred art. I am thinking of much work done in the Middle Ages. In many of these great works the artist uses abstraction because his ideas demand it. His objective was not to copy nature but to use it to stress our relationship to God, to digest the beauty of God's creation and glorify it. They tried to go *through* nature as a necessary step to God. They never minimized it. Also, it is a mistake to think that the artist in the Middle Ages did not study anatomy. In sketch books that have survived we see that artists did observe and study nature, including the human figure. Because artists are rooted in time and place, we should be suspect of the abstraction of the human body from any artist whose psyche has been formed in a heretical culture. In a Puritanical/Calvinist/Protestant/Muslim culture, for example, the body (as well as the rest of the physical world) is despised on some level and the artist absorbs this societal attitude. His 'belief' in abstraction has more to do with his inherent sense of the evil of the physical (his misunderstanding of the Incarnation) than any artistic philosophy. As long as the critic rejects the obvious modernist abstraction-meaning that the 'figure' does not even look human-the critic should not spend too much time worrying about this. This knowledge on the part of the critic is something that is developed through study, observation of works of art and especially his own drawing. It will become almost second nature; the critic will eventually be able to tell immediately whether or not the artist's abstraction is legitimate.

Anatomical Correctness vs. Realism

Two terms which are often used interchangeably but do not mean the same thing at all are **'anatomically correct'** and **'realistic.'** What's the difference between a work which is anatomically correct and one which is realistic? This is easy to understand if we think of a work by Michelangelo. He focused on anatomy; does anyone think his figures realistic? Focus on anatomy is a focus on what is essential to the human being. Focus on realism is a focus on what is accidental to the human being. The artist focused on anatomy will ask *"What is this"*; the artist focused on realism asks *"What does this look like"*? The accepted practice of two-dimensional artists working from photographs and sculptors using life casts which has developed in recent years is a result of a focus on realism and is an abomination.

These practices are yet another attempt to jump over time (circumvent reality) rather than go through it. When looking at paintings, question a focus on realism. In sculpture, always demand an over life-sized figure (or one smaller than life). One of the main reasons we confuse 'realistic' and 'anatomically correct' is due to the prevalence of illustrators working in the fine arts, outside of their area of expertise.

Note: The above refers to the fine artist only, not the illustrator. Again, an illustrator, who is by nature focused on realism, should not be creating figurative artwork for the inside of a church

4) <u>The Development of the Work</u>

Next in a work of art is the **Development** of the work. When looking at a work of art the viewer should have some awareness that the artist has gone through a process, a development, and has reached a conclusion. He (the artist) should be looking to make a statement, not ask a question. There should be a feeling of an idea thought out. This is another application of the use of traditional materials in fine art. The traditional media used in painting and sculpture lend themselves to this idea of development and growth.

One of the fundamental jobs of the artist is to lead the viewer. Not to control the viewer, but to lead him. This is a slow, gradual process The personal growth that the artist experiences while working on a piece in a *developmental* way is communicated to the viewer and is a primary source of this leadership. We must re-educate ourselves to be sensitive to this process of development because it takes time, and the appreciation of it also takes time.

Religious and sacred art are not to be glanced at quickly. They are forms of art that the viewer must be able to return to repeatedly. This means that it cannot just be an illustration of something. It should offer the viewer continual nourishment as he (the viewer) grows in spiritual development. In other words, the viewer should also be going through a process which should be facilitated by the work of art. As the job of the artist is to lead, not control the viewer, the work should be a companion to the viewer in his own process of spiritual growth and development. Hopefully this leads to the goal of a transformation into holiness. So how does the critic see or become aware of the artist's development? Here are some tips:

- Is the overall style of the work a bit *too* reminiscent of another period in history? Is the artist trying to make it 'look like' some particular style? (bad)

- Are there large areas, for example a leg or the sky, where there it is just an expanse-empty, rather than being another area developed through form, color or line? (empty expanse-bad)

- Do you sense that a *personality*, an *individual person,* made the work?

- When you look at the work a second and third time, do you see something new or see it differently? Notice new things? A work that has *developed* will continue to give us something no matter how many times we look at it. This is why it is essential for an artist to do the actual work himself. (good)

- Does the work suggest new things/thoughts to you or old things/thoughts seen in a new way? Or is it just an affirmation of something you already know? (new things- good)

- Do you get the idea that the work was done quickly? Is there only a suggestion, especially in a detail or a difficult part, instead of a search for the essence of it, for getting it right? (bad)

As the viewer/critic you need to be especially aware of a tendency which does no good in the criticism/ appreciation of art. That tendency is a desire we have in our culture to be hit with force when we look at something. If that 'need' to be 'wowed' is satisfied, we tend to let our attention wander, to give the thing less thought. This is a serious error of thought and one that does not lead to prayer or a transformation into holiness. It is very simple to counteract: just do not react to your first impression of a work. Not that your first impression is wrong-it may be right-but let some time pass and go back and look at the work a bit later. See slowly. Empty your mind. Be receptive. Remember all the elements of a work that need to be analyzed. Then criticize. (See Appendices 22, 23)

5) <u>The Conclusion of the Work</u>

Another element in a successful work of art is what I call the *Culmination,* or the *Conclusion* that has been arrived at by the artist. This follows closely on the heels of the development of the artist, but can be considered independently. First of all, you must ask yourself if a conclusion *has* been reached. What are the outward signs of a conclusion having been reached?

- Are the objects in the painting or the parts of the sculpture finished (good) or are they left undefined (bad), allowing the viewer to 'fill in the blanks? In other words, is the artist being definite? There is nothing indefinite in a finish.

- Do you have a sensation of being given a statement (good) or do you sense that the artist is reflecting the confusion he sees around him? (bad)

- Does the work end with a question mark? Does it raise questions within you (bad) or does it give you an answer (good)?

Even if you do not completely understand the statement or the conclusion of the artist, (or agree with it), you should have the sense that you are being given one. This most easily comes across in the form of strength in the piece. The critic must ask himself *"What is the artist trying to tell me?"* But, if he is open to an answer, he must get one. If the work does not supply one, or, strangely enough, if it is too obvious (that is, too superficial), it is not a successful work of art There is a contemporary idea which says the object of a work of art is to 'inspire the viewer to ask questions.' That is not true; this is an abdication of responsibility on the part of the artist. The object of a work of art is to give answers. They may be right or wrong, but they *are* answers. This is the reason behind knowing all of these characteristics of a work of art and having a basis for criticism. All of these aspects in the development of a work of art: The ideas, the composition, the technical expertise, the study of anatomy, are all areas that require a decision to be made and a conclusion to be reached. The making of these decisions along the way, so to speak, is necessary for the development of the final statement. The artist cannot skip over these and make a claim in favor of some 'idea' or 'intention' of the piece. In other words, it is an affirmation of the nature of our being: that we are both physical and spiritual, that we live in time and space and that this process ends in something that we now call the spiritual. It's called *telling the truth.* The job of an art critic is to make sure that the artist has kept to this. Left to himself, we see what happens. The artist goes the way of any fallen creature-to destruction of his own making.

(See Appendices 24, 25)

Sincerity, Fashion, Style and the Effect of Art History

We will now discuss some things that are mistakenly believed to be characteristics that should be considered when judging a work of art. Many artists and critics alike believe that a work should be judged: 1) by its level of sincerity; 2) by what other artists are doing or what 'ideas' are in circulation (fashion); 3) by how 'new' or how 'traditional' it is, that is, what it looks like (style); or finally, by how it fits into some sort of art evolution (art history). These are the key features in contemporary art criticism. I suppose it is ironic that they are the very things which the critic should never focus on. Perhaps this wrong-headed way of looking at art is due to the fact that all of these things are included in a successful work of art. All good art is sincere. All good art is new, as the successful artist is a person with his own personal vision. All good art has a style. And all good art takes its natural place in art history. But these are all a part of the thing but not a defining characteristic of the thing. They are a classic example of the difference between essences and accidents. All of these can be just as much contained in bad art as good, so let's look at them briefly and then leave them alone, and forget them when we judge a work.

Sincerity

The question of sincerity in art is complex. We know that any successful work of art was accomplished by an artist who was working with a sincere mind. We know this because God Himself told us *"Knock and the door shall be opened unto you."* Truth can only be reached by the sincere. So, what about unsuccessful works? Are all bad artists insincere? Well, not to put too fine a point on it, yes.

A problem with most viewers (critics) is that they 'believe' (assume) that the artist has sincerity. They then conclude that the work is good, that it must be good because the artist was so 'sincere.' But 'believe' in this sense has little meaning since it does not refer to an intellectual response to the examination of evidence, but rather to a superficial emotion. Why do we 'believe' the artist was/is sincere? Because he told us he was? Because of some predetermined and prejudicial 'feeling' on our part about artists who do religious work? It is exactly the other way around. First, we criticize the work. Only after an *objective* criticism can we conclude whether or not the artist was sincere.

It is *never* appropriate to focus on sincerity. It should not be spoken about because it is a question of the personal integrity of the artist himself and is a question for his conscience alone. If nothing else, it is bad form.

The issue of 'sincerity' is one of the reasons why art criticism is so important, especially in religious work. When we accept bad work because of what we perceive as the 'sincerity' of the artist, we are enabling his immorality. And yes, it is an immorality to be satisfied with doing inferior work, that is, to be insincere. If we participate in the modernist lie that virtue resides in one's feelings, we are rejecting the Truth of Christ. Sincerity, like faith, resides in the will and is an intellectual virtue. It is not emotional *and* we see it by its fruits.

Fashion

What is fashion? Fashion is what has taken hold of people's interest *at a given moment*. Its characteristics are flux and movement: changeability. It is by its nature superficial. It is all about a particular time, or moment, in history. That means it is by its nature an accident, not an essence. Therefore, it cannot be used as a basis for judging a work of art. Fine art stands in opposition to fashion. If art is a legitimate medium for saying something true about the nature of the universe, then it must always be concerned with deeper, eternal ideas. This, one could say, is to summarize the challenge to the artist: to be concerned with eternal ideas and to keep them *alive*, to always be trying to relate them to his *living* life. Anyone can repeat platitudes; the challenge is to rediscover them continually. This is a difficult one for the critic because sometimes we do not know if we are responding to the fashion or not. Again, we have help from the work itself. Fashionable work can usually be referred to as 'innovative' or 'relevant.' There may be a 'wow' quality but, on reflection, not much else. In a work based on fashion, the subject matter will be confusing. In the earlier section on the idea, we spoke of the artist who changes the story-that is, the actual facts of history. This would be an example of fashion in art. We also mentioned using photographs or life casts as a replacement for anatomical knowledge-a focus on realism. This would be another case of following the fashion in art. In other words, if the artist is taken with some fashionable idea, such as a new meaning for the Resurrection, for example, or that people now like 'realistic' art, he may succumb to the temptation of being part of the new fashion of the moment.

If the critic spends time meditating on the meaning of the subject before looking at the work, he will be more able to rise above the focus of fashion in it. Another help is to look at the work of a certain period, time, or moment, in history. Look at the inferior works of that period next to the successful. Also, look at works that were once thought great but that no one takes seriously anymore. They are 'dated'. The idea of *Fashion* as a temporary phenomenon becomes very obvious.

❖ *Tradition and Innovation*

Tradition is most often perceived as something dead and gone that we try to find meaning in. It is almost always seen as the past. The misunderstanding of this word is responsible for much of the bad art we see. Tradition should be a *living thing*. Pope Benedict XVI, in his book *The Apostles*, describes Tradition as "*not the transmission of things or words, a collection of dead things. Tradition is the living river in which the origins are ever present, the great river that leads us to the gates of eternity. And since this is so, in this living river the words of the Lord are ceaselessly brought about: "I am with you always, to the close of the age."* Innovation is the artist's fight against a misunderstanding of tradition. This is no more or less than the artist giving in to the sin of pride. It is interesting to look at artists on both sides of this same coin: those that misunderstand Tradition and 'follow' it, and those that misunderstand Tradition and are 'innovative.'

"Why do you seek the living among the dead? He is not here, but He has been raised."   -LK 24:5

Style

Style is connected closely to both fashion and art history. When an artist is focused on how he wants his art to look, which usually comes from a study of art history, he focuses on his **style**. Style is the predominating characteristic that art 'historians' use to designate a *school* or perhaps a *period*. It refers to the technique used by the artist or artists within a certain time frame and connects the technique to the ideas which concern the artist. This process is not connected to art criticism; that is, it is an analysis of some 'philosophy' or 'ideology' and analyzes the 'what' rather than the 'how.' Although ideas find expression in certain working methods and so are related to style, ideas are not the essence of style, which simply refers to that which makes a work look a particular way. One may speak of the Mannerist style or the Renaissance style, without any reference at all to the actual quality of the work. And that is the important thing to remember: artists are influenced by many things in their environment, just like anyone else.

When we look back in time, we can usually see similarities in terms of working methods and ideas of artists within a particular period of time. The artist does not belong to a separate species. He belongs to the human race and so the ideas which concern him at a given period usually pop up in other areas of whatever period we study. The fact that he may be concerned with an idea of his time does not mean that he is/was a great, or even a good artist (or a bad one). It just means that he is a human being, like everyone else. What is essential to remember is that this is a superficial characteristic and has nothing whatever to with the quality of the work; it is not something that anyone–either the artist or the viewer–should consider. We may be enamored of some particular period in art, but that is a personal preference, not the basis for an objective analysis/criticism of a work of art. Bad art as well as good can-and does-exist side by side in any given style. Unfortunately, because art 'history' taught by historicists is given such a prominent place in art education, many artists focus on style as if it were on the level of the previously discussed characteristics, i.e., an essence of a work of art. Indeed, many artists consider it the most important thing. Sadly, nowhere is this more tragic than in religious art. The reason is that the minute that an artist begins thinking *"What does it look like"* or *"How can this piece be classified"* he has stopped creating a work of fine art. Why? Because he (in this minimization of the significance of art) has decided to think on a totally superficial level. And since we understand the true purpose of art, we grasp the full tragedy of this.

We must differentiate between the focus on 'style' and an immersion in a philosophy which may result in a work conforming to a particular style. And the only way to do this is to forget 'style' and to criticize a work using the fundamental criteria of art criticism. The example of the icon comes to mind. One cannot look at contemporary icons without seeing immediately what is meant by mistaking style for content. The challenge to the contemporary icon painter which is so often met unsuccessfully is how to immerse oneself in a philosophy not compatible with the modern mind. So, the contemporary icon painter relies on making it 'look like an icon.' In other words, the contemporary artist who attempts to paint an icon is often an artist too concerned with the *style* of an icon to paint a high-level work of art. This becomes obvious if one looks at ancient icons. One surprise is the individuality of these icons despite having been painted within a particular 'style.' Contemporary icons, on the other hand, tend to look depressingly alike. The serious fine artist is not concerned with 'style.' He is too concerned with the principles of making a successful work to waste time on the unimportant. And this is the crux of the matter. The artist should be concerned with one thing and one thing only: how to make the best work possible based on *objective* criteria. The artist has enough to worry about keeping his mind on the essential. He has no energy to waste. It is perfectly fine for him to immerse himself in a way of looking at religious art and to follow his ideas. But any philosophy is not an excuse to forego the primary objective, which is to make a good work of art for the glory of God.

The preoccupation with style is a direct result of the relatively recent rise of the subject of 'art history.' It is an easy way to avoid the study of what makes for a good work of art. It is stressed by an intellectually lazy viewer and an intellectually lazy critic and made by an intellectually lazy artist. It is good to remember that a synonym of style is 'fashion.' Of course, we don't use this word because it exposes the truth about style: it is a passing fancy. It has nothing to do with truth. It has nothing to do with the true purpose of a work of art.

The Effects of Art 'History'

Art History, as a subject for study, is relatively new. It began at the end of the eighteenth century as a formal discipline, although Giorgio Vasari's *Lives of the Artists,* the basis for later art history, was written in the late 1500's (1578). This is very interesting, because the Renaissance was the beginning of the development of a temporal value system, when we began to compare ourselves to other men rather than to God. Art History, however it began, is today an invented, man-made construct. First of all, art cannot be looked at from some sort of historical perspective; as such it loses all meaning. We can certainly look at other subjects in terms of 'how did they develop'? Science, medicine, and mathematics are all subjects whose body of knowledge really does build upon what went before. But not art. By its very nature as a synthesis of personal experience, we must see that throughout human history, we have only good art or bad art. One artist does not 'build' on what another artist has said. Even in terms of technique it doesn't hold because artists are notorious for forgetting about or reviving techniques, depending on their needs.

There is another side to the study of art history which tends to destroy one's appreciation of art. The premise of the teaching of art history is that art is not a way to describe truths, but an activity that is an expression of the particular socio-political-economic setting of the artist in question, which is what is studied. Then the student is told how the artist was *influenced*! It *might* be allowed to rise to the level of journalism, if the artist was *really* important, or as a comment on a particular society, but nothing more. It so obviously becomes yet another way for us to apply contemporary, materialist philosophy that that one can only realize that this (this minimization of the importance of art) is what is intended.

The challenge to the critic is to look at a work of art as receptively and as simply as possible, rather as a child looks at things. If you need to know when the work was made in order to appreciate or analyze it, stop. You do not yet know enough to criticize it.

<u>*Part III*</u>

THE PROFANE IN SACRED ART

They posed this question to Him, "Teacher, we know that what you say and teach is correct, and you show no partiality, but teach the way of God in accordance with the truth. Is it lawful for us to pay tribute to Caesar or not?" Recognizing their craftiness He said to them, "Show me a denarius; whose image and name does it bear?" They replied, "Caesar's."
So He said to them: "Then repay to Caesar what belongs to Caesar and to God what belongs to God."

-LK 20:21-25

A Look at the Relationship between the Profane and the Sacred

Throughout Her history, the Church has repeatedly discussed and affirmed the importance of sacred art. We know why. The Church teaches the Truth and images, properly executed, are a search for Truth. So, we see and register the decline in the quality of sacred art with dismay. Some people fool themselves with some abstract theory of an artistic 'evolution', but in our hearts, we know this is a nonsensical view to take. Some try to explain bad art by saying that since the purpose of art was to 'educate' the illiterate, we don't need art anymore, we only need the 'ideas' that are expressed in art. Some try to cover the bad quality of a work of art through interviews or talks with the artist and tell themselves that the art must be good because of the impressive words of the artist. But again, in our hearts we know better. So, we either ignore (sort of) the issue (after all, art is just some pretty background that shows we're really 'Catholic'), or we ask ourselves continually what can be done. This, of course, describes the lucky ones. The rest sadly accept the substitution of mediocrity for excellence and just experience a general decline in their faith, without even knowing why Catholicism looks more and more like just another 'thing.'

The 'answers' to this decline in the quality of art are always given in the form of working backwards. We look at the fruits of high-level sacred art-the end points, describe them, and then use them to talk about 'what needs to be done;' in other words, as a starting point. For example, through a work of art we may experience transcendence into prayer, comfort, contemplation of the mysteries of God, an increase in faith, a sense of the reality of Truth. These things would be the end, or the fruits of high-quality sacred art. We then say: "Well, the artist needs to renew his inner life of faith, and then he'll make good sacred art." The artist then says to himself: "Well ok, I can do that." So, he goes to Mass and receives the Sacraments more frequently, increases his prayer life, *thinks* a lot about the *purpose* of sacred art (works on his intentions) but alas, his work does not get better. The reason is not (perhaps, and certainly not to be seen as *the* cause) his lack of faith. The cause lies in the fact that he is not doing what needs to be done artistically (physically). He is mistaking a result for a cause, which means he just goes around in circles. The cause of the decline of sacred art is due to the fact that we are not *working for the glory of God*. *"Wait a minute,"* you say, *"I hear 'religious' artists talking about their work all the time and no, you're wrong, they do want to glorify God. What do you mean they're not? Who are you to say such a thing?"*

If a furniture maker's chair continually falls over, would we tell him to go to confession to fix it? If your mechanic does not fix your car properly, would you tell him his faith is not sincere enough? Or, worse still, would you accept a chair that does not hold you up or a car that does not run because the person who made it is sincere in his faith? Do you think Joseph and Jesus were satisfied with badly fitted yokes? This is why bad art is not and never can be sincere. The worker is not at all sincere in looking *with humility* for the truth, that is, for the rules that will perfect his endeavor. Sincerity is the last thing on his mind. He is looking for some form of earthly 'success' (or some abstract notions of 'truth') and sadly that's easier to attain in the sphere of religious art by using non physical means (conceptualism) rather than physical ones. Which is easier for me, spending an hour telling you how much I know about anatomy, or spending a thousand hours in study and practice? It is especially acute and noticeable in the 'religious' artist because he has such a wealth of great and good examples to compare himself to and to learn from. What level of lying is going on in his mind if he sees himself on an equal footing with the great artists of the past? And when I say great, I am not speaking only about the famous of whom we have all heard. I'm talking about the thousands of unknown good and great works one can see in a thousand small churches or local museums all over Europe. I agree that in one sense, art is not the same kind of thing as a chair or a car. But in another sense, it is exactly the same kind of thing. And we cannot ignore the fact that when art was looked upon as the same kind of thing as a chair, we had much better art (and probably better chairs). When the *starting point* of the artwork was seen as a job to be done to the best of one's ability, *because one worked for the glory of God,* and the 'spiritual' or 'transformational' fruits of a work of art, that is, its *effects* on the viewer were seen as a gift from the Holy Spirit, given freely, *not a gift from the artist,* sacred art was truly sacred. (I remember as a child always having to put 'JMJ' at the top of every school paper. It was to remind us of Whom we were *truly* working for. Every artist should put it firmly in his mind before beginning any work).

A chair and a work of art are the same in their physicality; they both concern *things* in the created world, material, man-made, temporal things. This means that there are temporal rules and limits concerning them that must be obeyed. God created space and time and put us in them. The only way to glorify God properly is to work within these limits-His limits. Working within the rules and limits of our activity is the way we glorify God through our work. We can never glorify God by ignoring His limits for us. We can only offend God by devising our own rules (which in reality is working without regard to the very concept of rules) and then *requiring* or *expecting* His approval because we have done something to our own (or someone else's) satisfaction! And this is just what we are doing if we make a work of art with the intention of anything but glorifying God through our work. And *through our work* means exactly that, which is through the physical process and methodology involved in our area of endeavor. And we cannot, simply *cannot*, be sincere in our goal of glorifying God if we do not, with humility, accept and try to master the rules of our activity.

Simply put, if an artist wants to paint Our Lady but has not devoted at least some time and effort to learn anatomy, that artist cannot be working for the glory of God. Of course, we hope that our work has good results for the viewer but this *cannot* be our intention when making the work. If it is, we are working for man, not God. We are seeing ourselves as gods, rather than trusting that God will use our work as He sees fit.

Art is not the same kind of thing as a chair because the value of art cannot be measured solely in physical terms, in its functionality. (This complexity in art is precisely why the artist needs the critic).

By the way, the reason you would not accept a chair that falls over is that you know how to criticize the function of a chair. With practice and knowledge, you will soon be as familiar with a work of art as you are with a chair.

[The challenge of talking about the temporal effects of not having the love and glorification of God at the front and center of our work is that one opens oneself to the accusation of being a materialist, or being utilitarian, of thinking or having a value system based on the temporal, the material, of being accused of asking "Does it work?", rather than "Is it God's will?" This is just another aspect of a disunified mind. There are temporal and spiritual effects of not following the first commandment; it is not being a 'materialist' to

say so. I emphasize these temporal effects in total gratitude to God for showing them to us. It is out of His endless font of love and mercy that He gives us signs to guide us back to Him when we have strayed. Everything of course will 'work', if, and only if, it is done in accordance to God's will. The tree is indeed seen by its fruit.]

"Seek ye first the kingdom of God, and all else will be added unto you."   *-MAT 6:33*

The Decline in Critical Thinking

Criticism is measuring what has been done against an ideal-objective to the critic-and hopefully leads to positive change so that the work comes ever closer to the ideal.

Although most people would agree that criticism is somehow necessary in order to improve, contemporary thought is antagonistic to it. Proof lies in the fact that the very word 'criticism' has acquired a solely negative connotation. It is obvious that in a relativistic society criticism *is* negative. If there is no objective ideal or truth, then my criticisms are, in fact, negative attacks. As an art student I remember times when, in the face of an instructor's criticism, the student would respond with *"I wanted it that way."* The idea that the way he wanted it might have been wrong was completely alien to the student.

There are many contributors to this decline in critical thinking so necessary to the art of criticism, and the subsequent deterioration of art, but we must remember that there is a direct link to:

1. *The Protestant Revolt,* with its beginnings of relativism;

2. *Calvinism, with its beginnings of Puritanism and the evil nature of the physical; and*

3. *The response of the Catholic Church hierarchy during the Counter Reformation.*

Let's look at them one by one.

1)   *The Protestant Revolt*

The connection between Martin Luther and relativism is direct and clear. The concept of 'personal judgment' lays the groundwork for relativism. In his departure from the authority of the Church, manifested in both his rejection of the full Bible and his teaching of justification through faith alone (thereby severing faith from reason), Martin Luther laid the foundation for the rise of subjectivism. Then came its first fruit, the "Enlightenment." Kant defined enlightenment as *"Humankind's release from its self-incurred immaturity; immaturity is the inability to use one's own understanding without the guidance of another. Enlightenment is the process of undertaking to think for oneself, to employ and rely on one's own intellectual capacities in determining what to believe and how to act."* This did not lead to intellectual rot because there is anything inherently evil in using one's mind to accept the responsibility for one's beliefs, in fact this is a necessary job for the human being. Our intellect was given to us by God to assist us in working toward our salvation. No, intellectual degeneration began when we subjectified Truth. This in turn necessitated the notion of making the intellect subject to the emotions. Everything then becomes only itself and connected to nothing else because it is only the *Mind (the unit, the totality of the will, intellect, soul, and only lastly, the emotions)* that can unify us, because it is through the mind that we are connected to God. This rarely discussed truth of the 'Enlightenment' (which began at the fall of man but only given free reign after the Protestant revolt) has spread and grown until we have ceased thinking in a connected, unified way; we have become acclimated to 'thinking' (actually feeling) in compartments. We can no longer even look at a work of art and have a direct, correct response.

2) Calvinism/Puritanism

The theory of the total depravity of man and the subsequent theory of a predestination that results in the lack of belief in free will has led to more evils than we will examine here. And there is no need; just look at the society that surrounds us. In terms of criticism, we can see that if one believes in the impossibility of real improvement, criticism is useless. If man and the works of man are evil, if nature is separated from God's grace, one cannot be expected to create beauty. In fact, beauty, as a possible attribute of the works of man must be rejected out of hand. And so it has been among those with the taint of this philosophy within them.

3) The Response of the Counter Reformation

Keep in mind that the sometimes violent attacks on and negative responses to works of art/religious imagery have never said anything true about the evil of art; they rather affirm the significance of art. It is interesting to note that whenever there is a movement against images (and there have been such movements almost since the early days of the Church), it is always led by heretics: 1- the iconoclasts, who were rooted in or sympathizers to Aryanism, 2-Islam, 3- Protestantism. We may also include secular humanism to the list but I am not sure if it is accurate to classify it as a religion. These heretics realize on some level that they are being given something that they don't want to accept. After establishing a 'philosophy' based on tearing something apart, the last thing they want is to be shown that Truth is a synthesis which leaves *nothing* out. Iconoclasm is, in itself, a heresy.

What was the response of the Church hierarchy in terms of art at the Council of Trent? Basically, the Council outlined the teaching of the Church concerning images. This could have been a very proper thing to do. The problem was that the wording was imprecise, which led the way for 'clarification' after the Council. With this, artists were given a bit too much of a prescription for the way to make sacred art. So, what's wrong with that? (See Appendix 3).

To understand the whole picture, let us digress a bit. Contrary to popular belief, the artist does not possess a high degree of imagination. Imagination and creativity are *not* synonyms. Imagination is thinking up new things, maybe even impossible things; creativity is working within limits. The intertwining of these two words is the cause of much bad art.

The artist is an artisan. He works with his hands; he does physical work. An artist must possess a high level of creativity, which is needed to work within limits. Imagination, as a subordinate to creativity, can be a big help in this process, but can never be a starting point. People sometimes say about someone: "His imagination knows no limits." That is precisely why imagination must play a subordinate role in any artistic endeavor. There is probably more of a range of both intellectual ability and creativity in the art world than in other occupations (only because we do not truly embrace a Catholic culture), but any artist works best when he is told what to do. *What* to do, not *how* to do it. That distinction is extremely important and not respecting it leads to many problems. The challenge for the artist is to accept being told what to do while at the same time claiming his right to find his own way to do it. Looked at from the point of view of the critic (the person commissioning the work), *his* challenge is to respect creativity and ability of the artist while at the same time demanding that his high standards are met in the assignment he gives. The relationship is a back and forth one. The person commissioning the work sets the limits; the artist finds a way to work within them. This is the proper end for each, and there is an understanding that both are working toward the same end, each with his own role to play. But by the end of the Renaissance, when the artist claimed a position for himself that was unwarranted, this relationship became twisted. Affected by and giving in to the mindset of breaking down barriers as a way to claim 'freedom,' the artist began to demand the 'right' to do what he wanted, how he wanted. We know what happened: art deteriorated and became decadent (as it always does when the artist does not have a strict critic); this at the same time that the Protestant Revolt was in full swing, telling Catholics how evil images were anyway. Such was the situation at the Council of Trent.

We must remember that if some universal idea takes hold in a society at a particular point in history, it influences everyone-*everyone* in that society. No one is immune. And when people do not take the time to try to understand the whole idea and just see a part of it because that's easier, they tend to see themselves in an 'us' and 'them' situation, without realizing that all are thinking similarly, that is, *partially*. A proof of this in the contemporary world is seen easily by going into a newly built "Traditional" Catholic church and going into a "Novus Ordo" Catholic church. The artwork is equally bad and un-sacred in both, just in different ways, no matter the perspective. The only way to fight this and be on the outside, as much as possible, of *partial* current ideas is to try to understand an idea in its entirety and to accept that people with a 'part' of an idea are expressing ideology, not ideas. Only then can one try to be independent of it.

Anyway, at that time the big idea taking hold was the idea that freedom or bondage (limits) were things bestowed on man *from* man (and we all know that what was meant was the Church) and that this was a bad thing. No one examined the whole Idea of freedom, or limits, or even searched for a definition; they only saw a part. So, 'freedom' lay in tearing down walls, breaking out of limits. Why not? If limits are set by man, why not tear them down? Artists were especially prone to this due to a lack of the understanding on their part of the true nature of creativity, which demands working *within* limits. But was the hierarchy exempt from the influence of this way of thinking? I think not. The way they broke down limits was to make 'rules' for creating sacred art, to become too involved with the 'how-to' of making art. They knew what the result should be, and mistook it for the how. What was wrong was that both parties in the relationship-both the artist and the clergy-decided to work outside of the limits imposed by God, not man. The result was to separate intention from the physical process, a result that proved disastrous for art in the Church, and subsequently for the entire world.

The purpose of art is an arrival, a destination, a conclusion. Of course, we may know what that conclusion *should* be. But because it is an arrival, we can never be sure we'll get there until we get there. So although we may know what the conclusion *should* be, there is an element of suspense and uncertainty. We know the goal and do everything we can to reach it, but we can never be too sure, can never take the goal for granted. At any point along the way we can make a serious error and subsequently fail to reach our goal. What we do and the decisions we make along the way matter. In other words, in any endeavor, the methodology used is as important as the intention behind it. The methodology and the intention must act as a unit. One cannot separate them without compartmentalizing the thinking process. Or should we say that the fact of separating them is a symptom of an already compartmentalized mind. The clergy was able to direct the artist in terms of sticking to the goal of art, but the artistic methodology needed to succeed at this lay outside the area of the expertise of the clergy. That's why I say they broke down a limit.

Assuming success is the complacency that always accompanies the sin of pride. There is something about the movement through time which plays an essential part in reaching one's destination. Focusing on the 'inevitable' result (as long as we do certain prescribed things) causes us to jump over time, to ignore its significance, to disregard it. Of course, there are prescribed things to do and not to do. But it is in the performance, accomplishment, or avoidance of these things where the true responsibility and freedom of the individual lie. Making a work of art is not separate from life. The journey through it requires a moment-to-moment submission to God's will. We should be ready to change everything in a moment. It is an arrogance to talk about the result *in terms of something already achieved* before we get there. Over-emphasis on the result-and in fact seeing it as an *inevitable* result-changes our perspective. This change leads us away from God (away from Truth) not toward Him (toward the Truth). In fact, it leads to a kind of competition with God; we are setting ourselves up as a god. When Christ came into the world, He did not jump over time, He went through it.

After formalizing the purpose of art, the hierarchy began to see art as a tool. (Although I'm not sure which came first). Of course, it was and is a tool; everything is a tool *in God's hands*. Not in ours. The hierarchy of the Church should not have seen itself as the wielder of the tool, but rather as a fellow tool in the hands of God. Their approach was successful in the short term, but oh, how we are paying the price now.

In giving 'rules' and outlining steps to take for the making of a work of art which emphasized the end result of the work and the inner life of the artist, but had little or nothing to do with the physical working method, the clergy unknowingly set the stage for conceptualism-a kind of artistic gnosticism in which the physical reality of the work is diminished and the only important thing is the 'idea', which of course the viewer may or may not be privy to know or understand. The artist, thus armed with a much easier 'method' of making art and assured of success, became in that instant, artistically heretical. An ideologue. Someone working for the glory of man (in this case the Church hierarchy) rather than the glory of God. And our art, being separated from the truth, began to die.

Lastly, the hierarchy of the Church, in overstepping boundaries by telling artists how to create a work of sacred art, was participating in a relationship in which boundaries and limits were not respected but rejected. (There is a relationship between this and the development of the Baroque).

It is completely appropriate for the clergy to explore the challenges of making quality art in the Church with the artist. It is not appropriate for the clergy to try to explain how to make good art (unless he happens to be an artist as well) or use the artist as a tool in order to manipulate the laity. Soon he may find that he doesn't even need the artist at all; he can just get something cheaper from a factory (the American attitude).

Another un-looked for, un-wanted result in extending oneself outside one's proper boundary is that today an artist-who rejects *his* limits-can convince the hierarchy of any gobbledygook he wants to and the priest or bishop has no way to counter it (the European attitude). All the artist has to do is to convince the clergy that he followed the main rule set out by the Church Herself: good intentions backed up by faith. The actual work, the physical world, (the Incarnation) doesn't really matter anymore. Anyone who doubts this should visit the contemporary museum at the Vatican, not to mention almost any modern church. So, we see the immediate artistic fruits of operating outside of the nature God gave us, which can always be summarized as not glorifying God properly.

Let's see how this develops when it goes unchecked for a few hundred years. The fruits of the Church's (the hierarchy's) attitude toward art since the Counter Reformation are:

1. the completely justified disregard of the world toward the 'art' of the Church: She has gone from being understood as the source of Western art to being perceived as its greatest antagonist;

2. the inverted, topsy-turvy way of thinking of Catholicism: that the Catholic religion is un-creative and enslaving, while the secular world gives freedom;

3. uncounted numbers of lost souls due to the hypocrisy of teaching the truth in words and then contradicting it by surrounding the faithful with bad or non-art, which canonly lead people *away* from the truth by offering confusion and chaos, and trains minds which will be filled with impediments, not only to the actual truth, but to the very concept of the existence of truth;

4. the complete collapse of the quality of *all* art, sacred *or* secular.

WHERE WE STAND

When they sow the wind

They shall reap the whirlwind;

The stalk of grain that forms no ear

Can yield no flour;

Even if it could,

Strangers would swallow it.

-*Hosea 8:7*

A Summing Up

The combination of the above (relativism, Calvinism, abdication of the Church's responsibility to art) makes up the modernist cocktail and we are left with no basis at all for criticism. Instead, we stress the importance of the 'intention' or the 'idea' (both of which are jokes when used in this way) and if that can somehow be justified, then we cannot go farther. There is simply no basis. There may be an attempt to offer some sort of criticism based on results, but as the 'result' of art is difficult to pinpoint and since it *always* entails a synthesis of the physical and the non-physical, we are lost (due to having such a twisted relationship of the physical to the non physical.

The absence of or low quality of sacred images in our churches is a symptom of this way of thinking. The dogma of the Church has been reduced to a solely intellectual, 'top of the head,' one dimensional affair, something which can be expressed only in words (that have first been *written*). As such it is isolated and unconnected, and no longer touches the laity in a complete, unified way. There may be an emotional or an intellectual response from some, sometimes, but the holistic, transformational response characteristic of the knowledge of truth eludes us.

In deciding-either passively or aggressively-that the written word, read *or* spoken, is the most important medium, the only way to express Truth, we have summarily dismissed the Incarnation as well as Divine Tradition. And the result of this in artistic terms has been that for the first time in the history of the Church, the serious fine artist is seen as superfluous and rarely feels compelled to find artistic expression using religious themes: the main reason the fine artist generally lives on the 'outskirts' of society, producing meaningless junk for the rich. So, who's left to make 'art' for the Church? Craftspeople and illustrators, thereby depriving both the laity *and* the clergy (not to mention the rest of the world) of the real purpose and the real effects of fine art.

The Crisis of Superficiality

When you read the Gospel this Sunday, look around at the physical environment. The Gospel message that we read is connected to...what exactly? Expressed (incarnated) how and in what...exactly? When we look at it this way, we see the crisis: the crisis of superficiality. We need the artistic impulse of the fine artist alongside the liturgy: first, *simply because God has commanded it*; secondly, because of these things:

1. The artistic impulse exists because God created us in His image. We are *by God's command* creative beings. In developing this we are living in conformity to His will, if we do not, we are turning our backs on Him. We are made to know the truth through works of art. He Himself teaches us through works of art. Human artistic 'creation' is a manifestation of the human having been created in God's image. As such, we must realize and understand that it is as much a part of human nature as the power of thinking or the power of communication through speech. And as our words are always either confirming God's truth or denying it, so does our art. Art affects every single person, either being an influence of truth or a hindrance *to* truth.

   We must see and understand that if serious artists do not feel compelled to create high-level, serious works of sacred art, or if the clergy (and therefore the laity) accept inferior artwork, it means that *the truth is not alive in Catholic people*. Period. *"You are the salt of the earth. But what happens when salt loses its flavor?"* Well, we are beginning to see now whathappens. We must understand that our *appreciation* of art must come from *recognition*. The gauge of the quality of sacred art being made is the gauge of the state of the culture of the Church. If we do not try to tell the truth properly, that is, with an understanding of *all* of the ways and means with which this must be done, then the Incarnation, rather than being re-enforced as *the* historical Event that changed reality forever, is reduced to a quaint story told, a legend, with no real bearing on life. Creation as explained in the Bible is completely nullified. Nullify Creation and the Incarnation and what meaning can one give to Redemption and Salvation?

2. The Catholic is worshipping God in an anti-Catholic environment. How can the faithful be expected to follow dogma that appears disjointed from and in opposition to their very real-life experiences? Something is being asked of him which is impossible: to believe words and to follow teachings which are unrelated to the reality of his experience-including his experience at the moment he is listening to the Gospel. He is supposed to be learning about Truth while looking at superficial illustrations or non-art that fall far short of any truth. Regardless of his words, the priest who chooses bad art, non-art or illustrations in lieu of fine art for the inside of his church is telling and teaching people that the 'idea' or the 'intention' is the only thing that

matters. How long can the priest teach this untruth before his flock, believing what they are being told, put two and two together? What happens then? What happens then is the end of their belief in the Truth of the Catholic Church. Why be Catholic? Why not be something else, anything else? After all, homosexual 'unions' might be based on 'good intentions', so why not? An abortion might be based on 'good intentions', so why not? The Protestant church might have 'good intentions', so why not? Atheists might have 'good intentions', so why not?

Minimizing the actual physical world is a dangerous game that always ends in evil. Completely compartmentalized and disjointed thinking, which can only lead to minimizing the physical, is being affirmed and encouraged. In other words, the Church is assisting in the formation of minds that will have difficulty-to say the least-in grasping the whole concept of the existence of Truth, let alone its manifestation, which is the teaching of the Catholic Church. What possible good or value is there in ecumenism if we do not understand how to tell the truth? What level of schizophrenic thinking is at work when we elevate ecumenism to the highest activity while at the same time seemingly doing everything possible to cause people to leave the Church or-worse-cause rot from within? And speaking of ecumenism, what do we think the response of non-Catholics is (and I mean non-Catholics, as opposed to those who have already decided to join Her) when they see the low level of art and the non-art we put in our churches? Not being members of the 'choir' being preached to, they see it for what it is.

3. As people become more and more surrounded with visual images that lead them away from truth, art in the church must become more and more 'perfect' art, in order to 'combat' the secular. So instead of filling a church with bad imagery that tries to ape the secular by utilizing 'abstraction' or 'conceptualism' or with mass-produced, cheap, machine-made non-art items of no value (which says what about our value of Whom we are trying to represent), we must realize our duty to do something completely different. We must not sink to the level of the secular advertising industry by utilizing its method of using the visual image as a manipulative tool, but rather we must understand the significance of art by seeing it as God's tool which He will use as He sees fit. We cannot give Him second- or third-rate tools. We must decide to stop following Cain and try to emulate Abel. As such we must see the importance of art criticism. Serious art criticism is an expression of the

knowledge that art *always* either facilitates experiencing truth about the nature of the universe or *hinders* our understanding of the nature of the universe. It is not and never can be neutral. It is an essential adjunct to the liturgy because God has revealed this. The educated critic of art plays an essential role in the development of the creation of work that glorifies God. We cannot hope to have a serious body of *sacred* art unless and until we realize the significance of all fine art..

4. We must see that when the clergy itself cannot see the difference between accidents and essences-which must be the case when choosing machine-made non-art or low-level art for a church-they cannot make the laity understand the difference either. This is precisely why so many Catholics experience the tragedy of not believing in the Real Presence. They have no trust in the dogma of the Church because they have been given mixed, contradictory messages for too long. Good, honest sacred fine art in a church helps to make up the 'rich soil' in which the seeds of Truth are able to grow.

5. When people develop the habit of looking at low level works of religious art to the exclusion of good art, it predisposes them to feelings that may border on, or fall into, idolatry. They look at an 'image' but it does

not take them farther, or deeper. They either remain focused on the physical image, the 'thing' in front of them or they minimize it and spend their energy focusing on what the image represents. Either way they never have the transformational experience that can be the effect of a serious work of sacred fine art, and the relationship between the physical and the spiritual worlds becomes ever more twisted and dis-unified. If they entered a church and experienced the true value of a work of art, they would never be fooled into either/or thinking: either the 'thing' is all there is or the 'thing' is just an illusion. Perhaps then there would not be so many Catholics turning to Eastern philosophies like Buddhism.

6. The entire reality of the Catholic Church is that She offers something unique to people, something they cannot get from any other source. That message should be present and alive in each and every Catholic Church building. Having fine art (unique and individual pieces of art that must be seen to be appreciated) inside of a church building, that is, having something physical inside of a church that you cannot see unless you enter that church, is a metaphor for the message of the Church. It doesn't have to be the reason that people go into the church

building-although there are many, many examples of just that all over the world-the point is that if they want to see *that* particular thing they must go into *that* particular church. Like it or not, they will not be able to find it anywhere else. And the *'that'* we are talking about should be nothing less than a sincere search for Truth. Whatever is experienced on the outside, inside of a Catholic church there must be only truth as the aim and purpose. Because we know that this will lead to the ultimate *That*: God. But if the laity go into a church and see things that are impersonal, badly done or mass-produced-in other words, things they can find anywhere, anytime, outside or inside of any other church, in any religious supply shop *or* any secular building-what is the message being given (and received)? Simply this: that there is nothing unique in the Catholic Church, it's just another 'church.' It only gets worse if what they can see outside is done better!

7. We can truly understand the contemporary crisis in the Church if we contemplate the significance of the hierarchy's lack of awareness of all of the means at its disposal for giving the truth-or its opposite-to the faithful. In other words, if the priest sees the truth as something *written,* to be expressed solely in words, or, if he believes in the 'neutrality' of visual images, can he himself have a deep understanding of truth?

The priest can easily test his own beliefs and values by asking himself some simple questions. How does he categorize the importance of things in his church? He must, for example, have a roof that doesn't leak and toilets that flush, but how does he approach the challenge of the importance of placing visual images inside the church? How much thought does he give to this most important thing? Is it essential or is it something he adds, after all the 'important stuff' is done?

One Last Thing

One question remains to be answered. Is there no place for personal opinion in art criticism? Is our own point of view to be stifled in the name of a set of rules? The answer to this is both yes and no. Because we live in a time which glorifies personal 'opinion,' it is somewhat difficult to accept the fact that an uneducated and undeveloped 'opinion' has very little value and that it *is* possible to like the wrong things. And there *are* rules in art. So, in a sense no, there is no place for the personal in art criticism. But in another sense, there is value in personal opinion and it can be legitimate. In fact, it can add depth and richness to experiencing a work of art. When? When we have mastered the objective rules of art and can offer serious criticism based on these and we have decided that in terms of artistic excellence there is little difference between two or three artists, then we may have a favorite based on personal appeal, which may be worthwhile. (For example, I have often gone back and forth about who is the better sculptor: Donatello or Michelangelo). One must be able to offer an individual viewpoint that embroiders upon the general understanding of an artist. This is the value of an 'opinion.' Sharing this opinion has much value in that it can expand another's experience of a work of art by adding the gift of another objective (from someone else) viewpoint.

Or, we may have a deep, positive response to what can only be called bad art, knowing full well that it is bad. I am deeply attached to a number of works of art for completely personal reasons and would never dream of calling them great, or even good works of art. They have personal, sentimental meaning for me. Each one tells a personal story. I keep them in my house but I would never put them in a public place such as a church or a museum. Doing so would take them out of the realm of the personal and be a statement that these works should be appreciated by all, giving them an objective artistic significance which they do not have.

Also, keeping mass-produced religious images in one's home is not only perfectly acceptable, but important. But the value in having these reproductions in one's home can only be experienced if one sees something *qualitatively* different when one enters a church. The repeated immersion in an environment with serious fine art will not only serve as immunity against idolatry but will reinforce the purpose of art. This will serve to reinforce the significance of the representations in the home.

Hopefully, learning that there is objectivity in art, as in everything, and that there are learnable rules to apply, will not turn us into artistic prigs or snobs. Remember: do what you like in your own house, but also remember that a church is not your house, it is God's house.

And remember to keep in mind also that the line which is crossed which makes the difference between a good or competent work of art and a great one lies in the personality of the artist and so lies outside of the critic's expertise and control. It is the inner life of the artist which makes *that* difference, but the critic should remember that one way to help the artist on his journey is through legitimate and serious art criticism.

The critic has an awesome responsibility.

APPENDICES

APPENDIX 1

Note on Visual Appendices: None of these images is identified but I promise you that all of the contemporary church interiors are authentic, that is, pictures of real church interiors, and the pictures of the contemporary buildings are really cathedrals.

First let's look at some examples of iconoclasm committed by enemies of the Catholic Church.

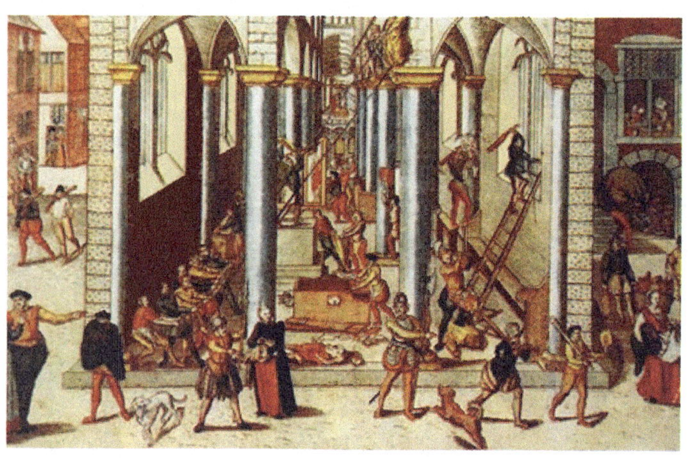

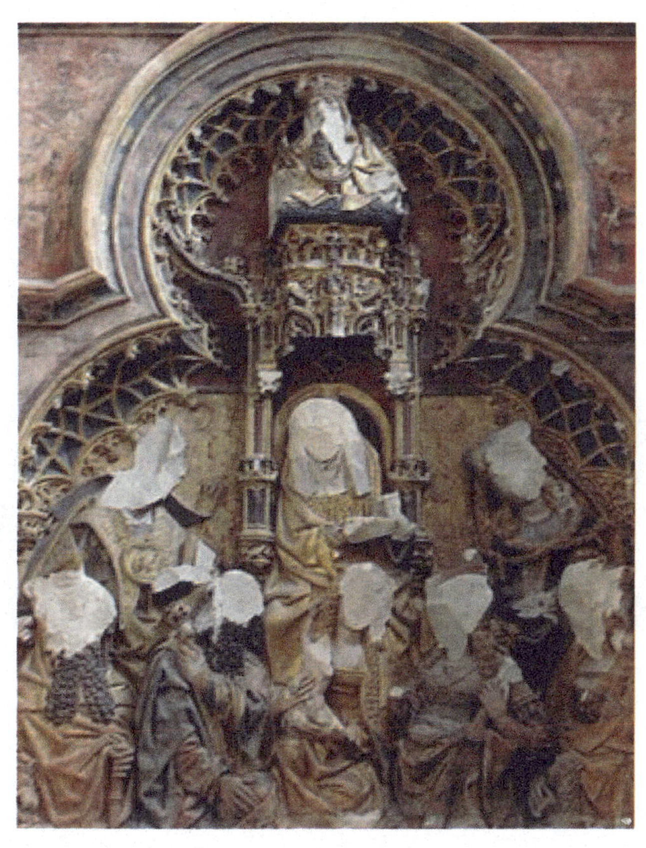

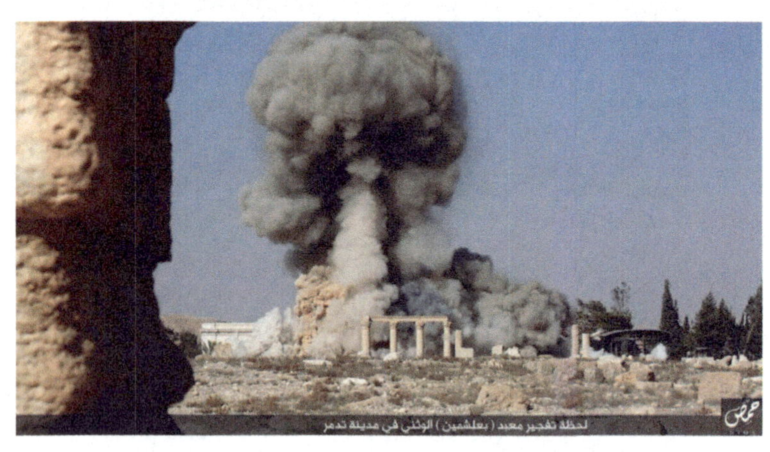

98

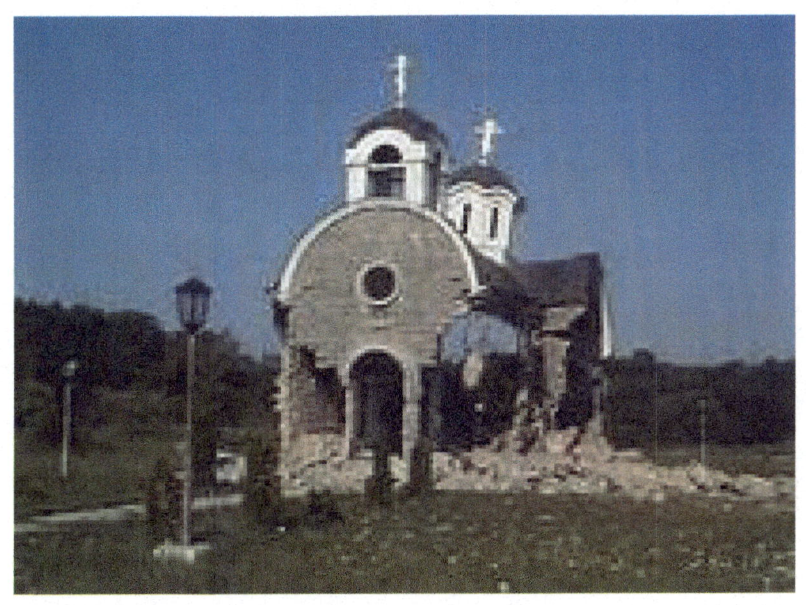

APPENDIX 2

Now let's look at some examples of iconoclasm committed by Catholics themselves.

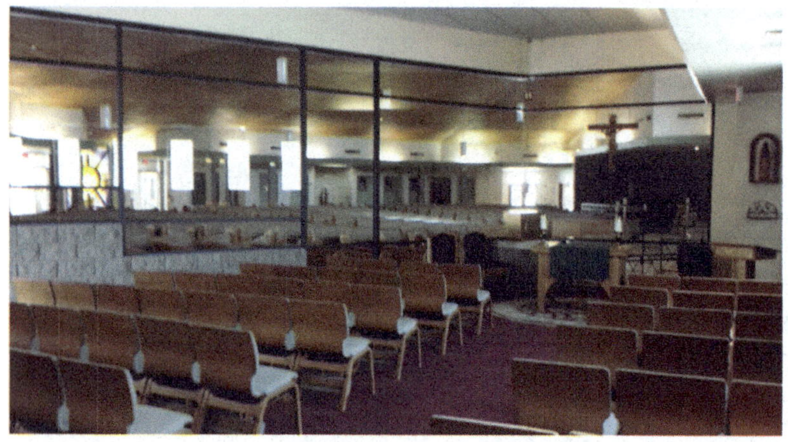

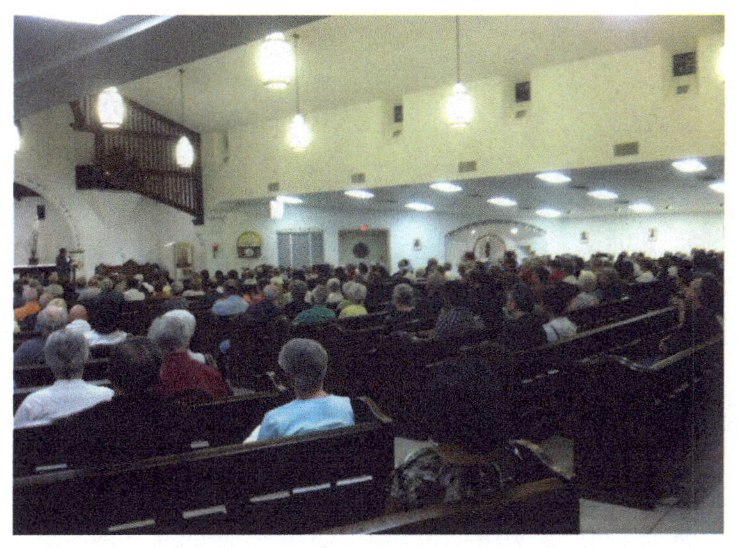

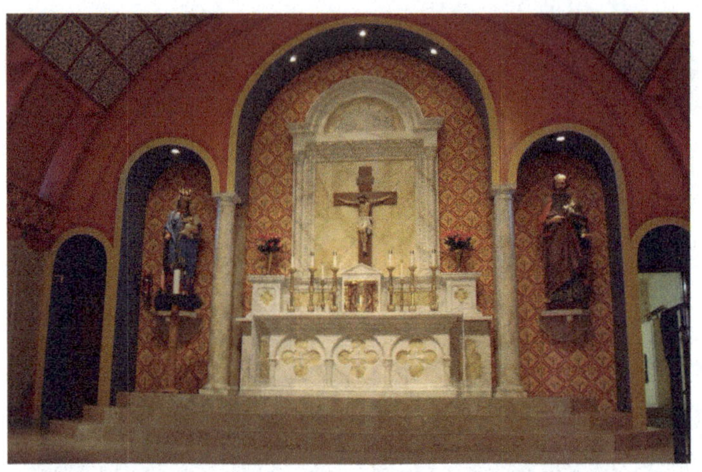

All work in the above church is machine-made, mass-produced. The altar is painted to 'look like' marble. An iconoclastic abomination.

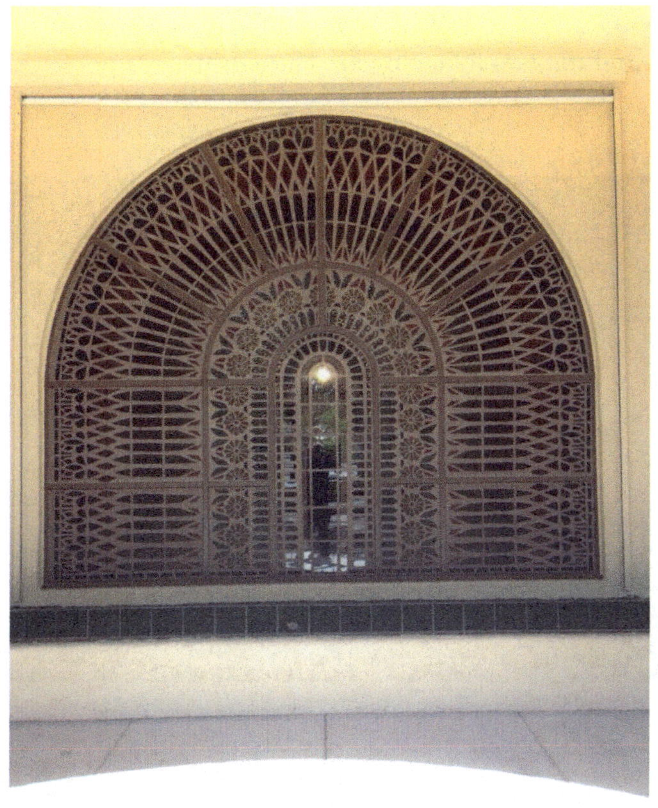

Yes, it is the door of a Catholic church, not a mosque.

This and the two following are cathedrals:

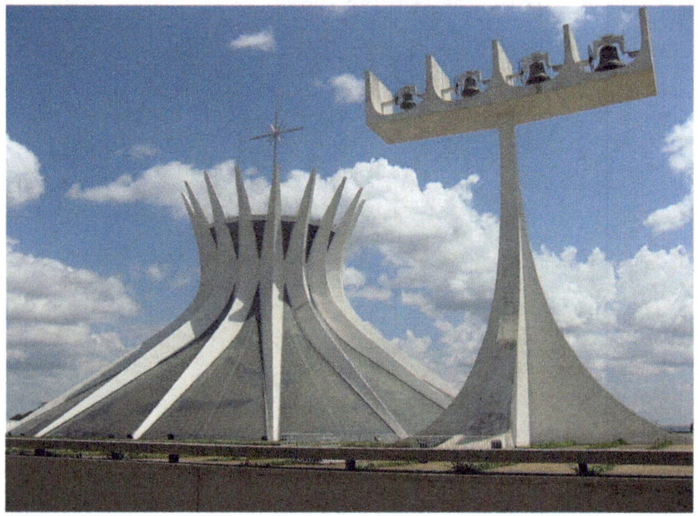

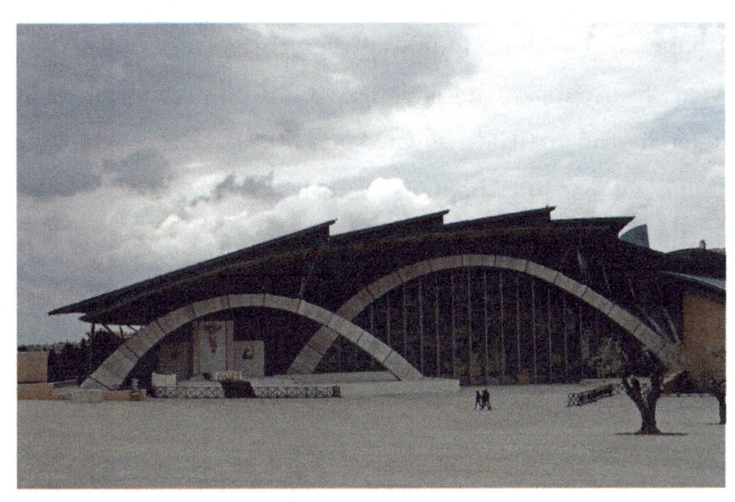

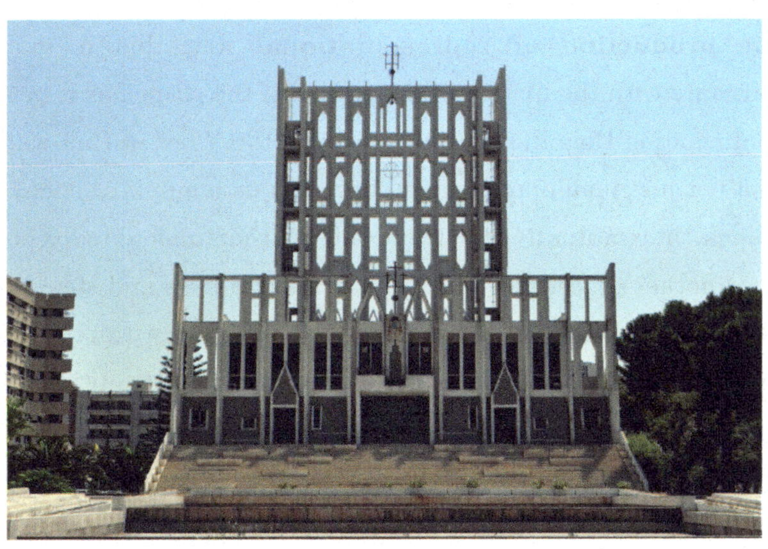

APPENDIX 3

I have chosen these four writings, three from Councils and one Encyclical, because they span over 1200 years and show the changes in the attitude toward art in the Church very clearly. Although I have put them in historical order, my notes contrast: *first,* the Second Council of Nicaea to the Sacrosanctum Concilium of Vatican II; then *second,* The Council of Trent to Musicae Sacrae.

Second Council of Nicaea - 787 A.D.

To summarize, **we** declare that we **defend** free from any innovations **all the written and unwritten ecclesiastical traditions that have been entrusted to us. One of these is the production of representational art**; this is quite in harmony with the history of the spread of the gospel, as it provides confirmation that the becoming man of the Word of God was real and not just imaginary, and as it brings us a similar benefit. For, things that mutually illustrate one another undoubtedly possess one another's message. Given this state of affairs and stepping out as though on the royal highway, following as we are the God-spoken teaching of our holy fathers and the tradition of the Catholic Church —for we recognize that this tradition comes from the Holy Spirit who dwells in her—we decree with full precision and care that, like the figure of the honored and life-giving cross, the revered and holy images, whether painted or made of mosaic or of other suitable material, are to be exposed in the holy churches of God, on sacred instruments and vestments, on walls and panels, in houses and by public ways, these are the images of our Lord God and Savior, Jesus Christ, and of Our Lady **without blemish**, the Holy God-bearer, and of the revered angels and of any of the saintly holy men. The more frequently they are seen in representational art, the more are those who see them drawn to remember and long for those who serve as models, and to pay these images the tribute of salutation and respectful veneration. Certainly, this is not the full adoration {latria} in accordance with our faith, which is properly paid only to the divine nature, but it resembles that given to the figure of the honored and life-giving cross, and also to the holy books of the gospels and to other sacred cult objects. Further, people are drawn to honor these images with the offering of incense and lights, as was piously established by ancient custom. Indeed, *the honor paid to an image traverses it, reaching the model*, and he who venerates the image, venerates the person represented in that image. So it is that the teaching of our holy fathers is strengthened, namely, the tradition of the Catholic Church which has received the Gospel from one end of the earth to the other. So it is that we really follow Paul, who spoke in Christ, and the entire divine apostolic group and the holiness of the fathers, clinging fast to the traditions which we have received. So it is that we sing out with the prophets the hymns of victory to the Church: Rejoice exceedingly O daughter of Zion, proclaim O daughter of Jerusalem; enjoy your happiness and gladness with a full heart. The Lord has removed away from you the injustices of your enemies, you have been redeemed from the hand of your foes. The Lord the King is in your midst, you will never more see evil, and peace will be upon you for time eternal.

Therefore **all those who dare to think or teach anything different**, or who follow the accursed heretics in rejecting ecclesiastical traditions **or who devise innovations,** or who spurn anything entrusted to the Church (whether it be the Gospel or the figure of the cross or any example of representational art or any martyr's holy relic), or who fabricate perverted and evil prejudices against cherishing any of the lawful traditions of the Catholic Church, or who secularize the sacred objects and saintly monasteries, we order that they be **suspended** if they are bishops or clerics, and **excommunicated** if they are monks or lay people

Anathemas concerning holy images:

1. If anyone does not *confess* that Christ our God can be represented in His humanity, let him be **anathema**.
2. If anyone does not *accept* representation in art of evangelical scenes, let him be **anathema**.
3. If anyone does not *salute* such representations as standing for the Lord and His saints, let him be **anathema**.
4. If anyone *rejects* any *written or unwritten* Tradition of the Church, let him be **anathema**.

Council of Trent, Session the 25th, *ON THE INVOCATION, VENERATION, AND RELICS, OF SAINTS, AND ON SACRED IMAGES*, 1563:

And if any abuses have crept in amongst these holy and salutary observances the holy synod earnestly desires that they be utterly abolished; in such wise that no images conducive to false doctrine, and furnishing occasion of dangerous error to the uneducated, be set up.

In fine, let so great care and diligence be used herein by bishops, *as that there be nothing seen that is disorderly, or that is unbecomingly or confusedly arranged, nothing that is profane nothing indecorous, seeing that holiness becometh the house of God.* (my italics).And that these things may be the more faithfully observed, the holy synod ordains, that it be lawful for no one to, place, or cause to be placed, any unusual image in any place, or church, howsoever exempted, except that it shall have been approved of by the bishop: also, that no new miracles are to be admitted, or new relics received, unless the said bishop has taken cognizance and approved thereof; who, as soon as he has obtained some certain information in regard of these matters, shall, after having taken advice with theologians, and other pious men, act therein as he shall judge to be agreeable to truth and piety. But if any doubtful, or difficult abuse is to be extirpated; or, in fine, if any more serious question shall arise touching these matters, the bishop, before he decides the controversy, shall await the sentence of the metropolitan and of the bishops of the same province, in a provincial council; yet so, that nothing new, or that has not previously been usual, in the Church, shall be decreed, without the most holy Roman Pontiff having been first consulted.

24. The ordination and direction of man to his ultimate end - which is God - by absolute and necessary law based on the nature and the infinite perfection of God Himself is so solid that not even God could exempt anyone from it. This eternal and unchangeable law commands that man himself and all his actions should manifest and imitate, so far as possible, God's infinite perfection for the praise and glory of the Creator. Since man is born to attain this supreme end, he ought to conform himself and through his actions direct all powers of his body and his soul, rightly ordered among themselves and duly subjected to the end they are meant to attain, to the divine Model. Therefore, even art and works of art must be judged in the light of their conformity and concord with man's last end.

25. Art certainly must be listed among the noblest manifestations of human genius. Its purpose is to express in human works the infinite divine beauty of which it is, as it were, the reflection. Hence that outworn dictum "art for art's sake" entirely neglects the end for which every creature is made. Some people wrongly assert that art should be exempted entirely from every rule which does not spring from art itself. Thus, this dictum either has no worth at all or is gravely offensive to God Himself, the Creator and Ultimate End.

26. Since the freedom of the artist is not a blind instinct to act in accordance with his own whim or some desire for novelty, it is in

no way restricted or destroyed, but actually ennobled and perfected, when it is made subject to the divine law.

27. Since this is true of works of art in general, it obviously applies also to religious and sacred art. Actually, religious art is even more closely bound to God and the promotion of His praise and glory, because its only purpose is to give the faithful the greatest aid in turning their minds piously to God through the works it directs to their senses of sight and hearing. *Consequently, the artist who does not profess the truths of the faith or who strays far from God in his attitude or conduct should never turn his hand to religious art. He lacks, as it were, that inward eye with which he might see what God's majesty and His worship demand. Nor can he hope that his works, devoid of religion as they are, will ever really breathe the piety and faith that befit God's temple and His holiness, even though they may show him to be an expert artist who is endowed with visible talent. Thus, he cannot hope that his works will be worthy of admission into the sacred buildings of the Church, the guardian and arbiter of religious life.*

28. *But the artist who is firm in his faith and leads a life worthy of a Christian, who is motivated by the love of God and reverently uses the powers the Creator has given him, expresses and manifests the truths he holds and the piety he possesses so skillfully, beautifully and pleasingly in colors and lines or sounds and harmonies that this sacred labor of art is an act of worship and religion for him. It also effectively arouses and inspires people to profess the faith and cultivate piety.*

29. *The Church has always honored and always will honor this kind of artist. It opens wide the doors of its temples to them because what these people contribute through their art and industry is a welcome and important help to the Church in carrying out its apostolic ministry more effectively.* (my italics).

CONSTITUTION ON THE SACRED LITURGY SACRO SANCTUM CONCILIUM, 1963

43. Zeal for the promotion and restoration of the liturgy is rightly held to be a sign of the providential dispositions of God in our time, as a movement of the Holy Spirit in His Church. It is today distinguishing mark of the Church's life, indeed of the whole tenor of contemporary religious thought and action. So that this pastoral-liturgical action may become even more vigorous in the Church, the sacred Council decrees:

44. It is desirable that the competent territorial ecclesiastical authority mentioned in Art. 22, 2, set up a liturgical commission, to be assisted by experts in liturgical science, sacred music, art and pastoral practice. So far as possible the commission should be aided by *some kind* of Institute for Pastoral Liturgy, consisting of persons who are eminent in these matters, and *including laymen as circumstances suggest.* Under the direction of the above-mentioned territorial ecclesiastical authority *the commission is to regulate pastoral-liturgical action* throughout the territory, and to promote studies and necessary experiments whenever there is question of adaptations to be proposed to the Apostolic See. (my italics).

45. For the same reason every diocese is to have a commission on the sacred liturgy under the direction of the bishop, for promoting the liturgical apostolate.

Sometimes it may be expedient that several dioceses should form between them one single commission which will be able to promote the liturgy by common consultation.

46. *Besides the commission on the sacred liturgy, every diocese as far as possible should have commissions for sacred music and sacred art.*

AUTHOR'S NOTES

1) *The Second Council of Nicaea, 787 and Sacro Sanctum Concilium, 1963*

When we read the above documents, it is very easy to see the steady decline in sacred art. We begin with: *"If anyone does not accept representation in art of evangelical scenes, let him be **anathema**"* and we get to: *"every diocese, as far as possible, should have commissions for sacred music and sacred art."* In other words, in 787 we 'rejoiced exceedingly' to have the enemies of what had been *"entrusted to the Church"* be crushed. We exalted that we were again ready to openly *"follow Paul, who spoke in Christ, and the entire divine apostolic group and the holiness of the fathers, clinging fast to the traditions which we have received"* [traditions including images-*author's note*]. In 1963 we didn't even see the need to be concerned with art directly and personally at all, just put it in the hands of a "commission." The very words of the directive serve as proof that the writer of the directive neither knew nor understood art or the creative process and was completely un-qualified to discuss the matter at all. The very words 'art commission' put together make up an oxymoron. The creation of any successful commissioned work of fine art can only happen in a relationship made up of *no more* than *two* individuals: the patron and the artist. Period. It is not and can never be a group effort of any kind on either side. The reason is simple. The minute a group of people, of any kind, exist *as a group*, their mentality undergoes an immediate change. They may or may not be aware of this change, but it is a reality nonetheless. The change is that each 'individual' in the group gives up a little (or a lot) of his 'individuality' to the 'good' of the group. There then exist two focuses: the focus on 'consensus' and what naturally becomes the lesser focus: art. The fact is that the critic, who would also be the patron, and the artist are *both,* or should I say, *each,* engaged in his own highly creative act.

2) <u>*The Council of Trent, 1563 and Musicae Sacrae, 1955*</u>

By the Council of Trent, a change has come: The Church has developed not only Her patronage of art, but also Her position as critic of art. This is natural and proper; throughout this book I have used the word 'critic' along with patron, to describe simultaneous jobs. The challenge is that, as they are simultaneous jobs, both must *develop* simultaneously; one does not automatically become a better critic just because one has commissioned more artwork. The criticisms are good and valid: *"that there be nothing seen that is disorderly, or that is unbecomingly or confusedly arranged, nothing that is profane"* in a church is indeed excellent criticism. (It's hard to believe how we ignore this today). Unfortunately, the hierarchy took this criticism and made the mistake of seamlessly transferring it to the 'how' of making an image rather than realizing it was the 'what.' This is understandable. They knew the *'what.'* I just often wonder how things might have developed in the Church if the hierarchy had instead realized that yes, artists had been going astray, but the way to redirect was to remind them (as well as themselves) of the challenge of limits, and the joy and immense creativity possible when working within them.

Which brings us to 1955, when the severance between the physical and the spiritual, the theory and the performance, is complete. Pope Pius XII takes it for granted that only a Christian should make sacred art. 'Non-religious' artists should not; *"Nor can he hope that his works, devoid of religion as they are, will ever really breathe the piety and faith that befit God's temple and His holiness, even though they may show him to be an expert artist who is endowed with visible talent."* It's not that I do not understand what he was trying to say. But I do wonder if *he* knew what he was *actually* saying.

When we deconstruct an idea, without completing the work of re-unifying it, we are forming an ideology, a part of a whole. When we isolate *part* of an idea-in this case the inner life of the artist, which is only part of the *Idea* of sacred art (even smaller than a part, a part of a part) we are focusing on something smaller than the *Idea* and forming an ideology. We are using our intellect and our words to turn something sacred (from God) into something profane (worldly). And because the smaller can never encompass the larger, a part of an Idea can never represent the truth about any Idea. The part cannot encompass the whole. Pope Pius XII took for granted the complete secession of the physical from the spiritual, the material from the immaterial, the methodology from the intention, and after doing this he *jumped* to the conclusion that a part of the immaterial was the whole! This cannot be (for us) as long as we exist in space and time. One cannot understand art and say *"his works" ..." will (n)ever breathe piety and faith...even though they may show him to be an expert artist."* As I have stated, the Idea is the backbone of any work. If the Idea is lacking-for whatever reason-the work is not good and should never be placed in a church. If the artist is shown to be an "expert artist"-which is possible only through valid artistic criticism, and since valid artistic criticism is *only* possible with a thorough evaluation of the *Idea*-all aspects of the Idea-as well as the material elements in a work, the statement has no meaning. An artist can be a self-identified devout Catholic and have bad artistic ideas (be a bad artist). Let me say that again: *An artist can be a [self-identified] devout Catholic and be a bad artist.*

This encyclical lays the groundwork for both Conceptualism in art and the relativist philosophy in which any criticism of anything is impossible. It is a perfect example of why we cannot take art for granted, cannot see it as a thing 'built upon,' can *never* have a superficial attitude to it. Art presents the greatest challenge of all: the challenge of being and staying alive, of living every moment anew. When we have a *theory* of art rather than the *practice*, we are dead. We remain alive by following the proper order: first, the work is criticized. If it has been found successful, then we may possibly make assumptions about the artist's religious state, if we dare. If, having criticized the work on its artistic merit and found it unsuccessful, we just leave it alone. There is no need to make any commentary on the artist's faith. He may be a self-identified devout Catholic; he may not. Frankly, that is between him and God, and the proper place to deal with it is in the confessional, not in the artwork.

Note on the following visual appendices: I have not identified any of the works by title, artist, or location. This is because I want you to focus solely on the visual impact of the work itself. Some works will be instantly identifiable; these I would encourage you to see in person if possible or to look up so that you can see the image better and larger.

Also please realize that the unsuccessful works that I have chosen can be criticized much more broadly than I have done. (An unsuccessful work of art always has more than one thing wrong with it). My purpose was to focus on just one characteristic at a time. In the homework assignment at the end I have given you the opportunity to criticize a work completely, taking into consideration all of the characteristics I have covered.

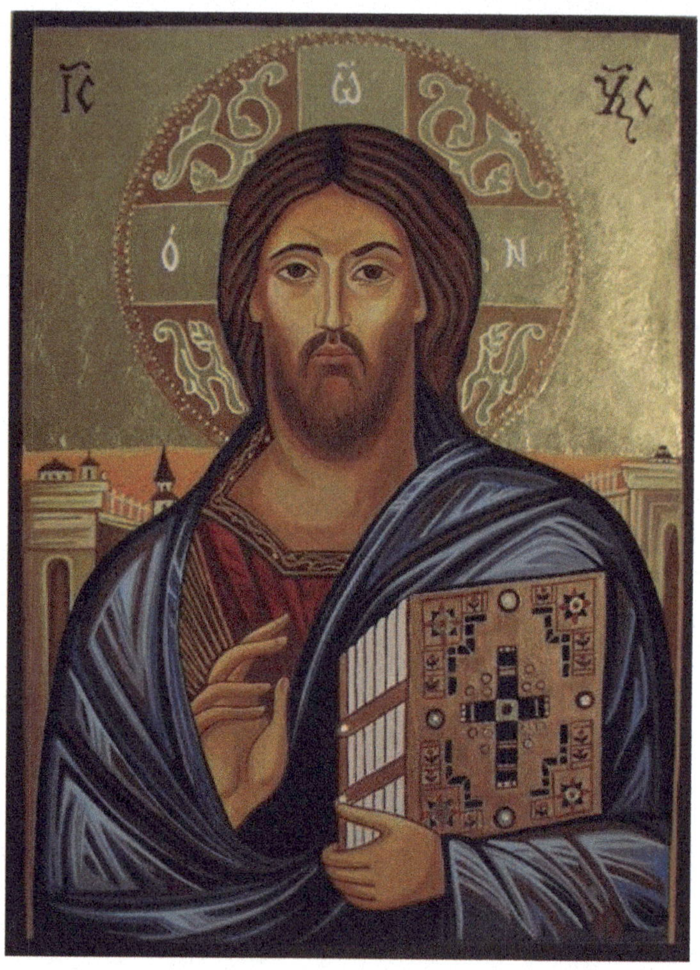

This is an illustration, not a work of fine art. It is not an icon; it *looks like* an icon. There is no attempt to model any forms, to study and describe the *body* of Christ. The body parts are all flat and what should be modeled, that is, what should have been studied as an essential characteristic of the humanity of Christ, has been reduced to superficial stripes and shapes-a pattern. There *is* a pattern to the human body, but what is *essential* to the human body is that it is a form; it exists in three dimensions (time *and* space). This entire image is flat and two dimensional. It is an illustration because it is made up of 'facts' alone. These facts tell us that there is a head, a hand, etc., but no searching for the essence of what a hand is made up of, and therefore no truth about a hand. An artist can never hope to reach the truth about the human form if he makes it completely flat, without indicating volume. An artist is not telling the truth about Christ if he works in this way. Christ was fully divine AND *fully* human. The danger of putting these kinds of illustrations in a church is that the viewer (and the clergy) is paying no heed to the Truth of accidents and essences. How can they believe in the Real Presence? This painting looks as though it was painted for believers in Docetism. It is simply not telling the truth. Period.

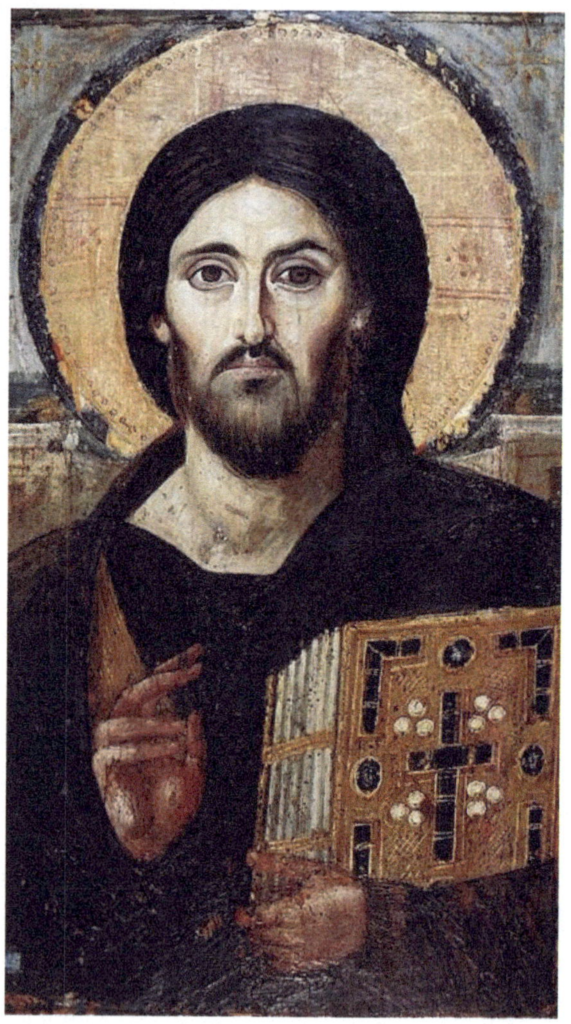

This is an icon, a work of fine art. In this image we see the truth being told: that Jesus Christ was fully God and fully human. The artist has considered the human form and painted the human figure with volume; we can sense the body under the material. The neck is a strong, full form. The hands are simply beautiful; Christ's left hand is really holding that book. The face is a marvel of form expressed in two dimensions. The artist used color with the knowledge that it had a purpose: the purpose of describing something true and essential about his subject. The viewer of this painting can never walk away with the impression that the body of Christ was an illusion. It is not only a painting of God; it is also a painting of a man.

It is a masterpiece: the union of the physical with spiritual.

APPENDIX 6: THE DIFFERENCE BETWEEN ILLUSTRATION AND FINE ART (III)

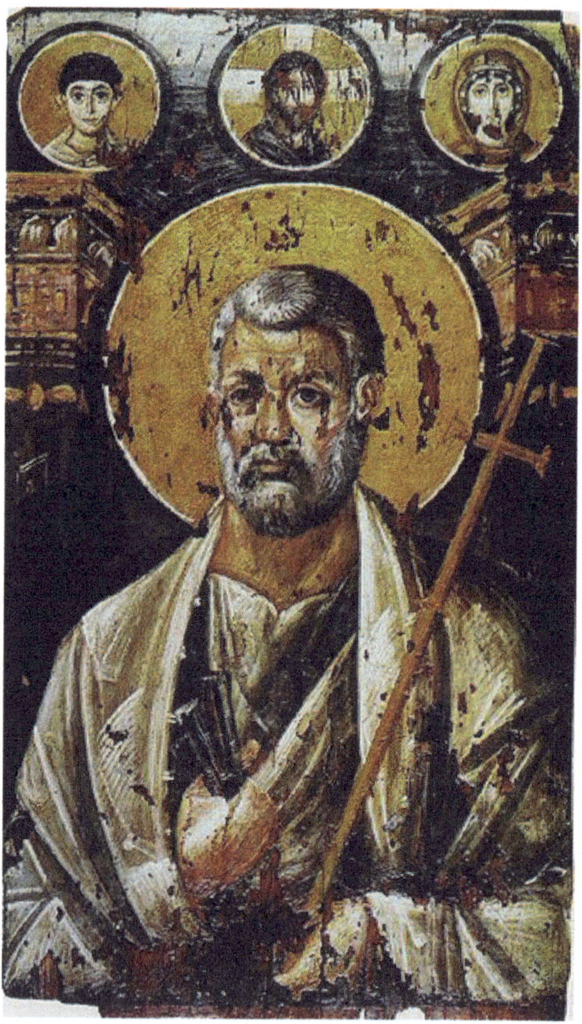

This is also an icon, a work of fine art.

Look at the way the artist modeled all of the bodily forms. The viewer can tell that this was an artist in love with the created world. You don't have to be told that this is St. Peter.

It was done in the 6th century so one cannot say he had the advantages of the modern world in terms of anatomical knowledge.

Another masterpiece. I would like to have you notice the individuality of these two icons. The artists were not following a 'formula'. They were not mistaking the symbolism for the essence of a work of fine art. Neither looks as if the artist were doing a paint-by-numbers page. Each work is a new statement; these magnificent works do not have the feeling of being stamped out which contemporary icons all seem to have.

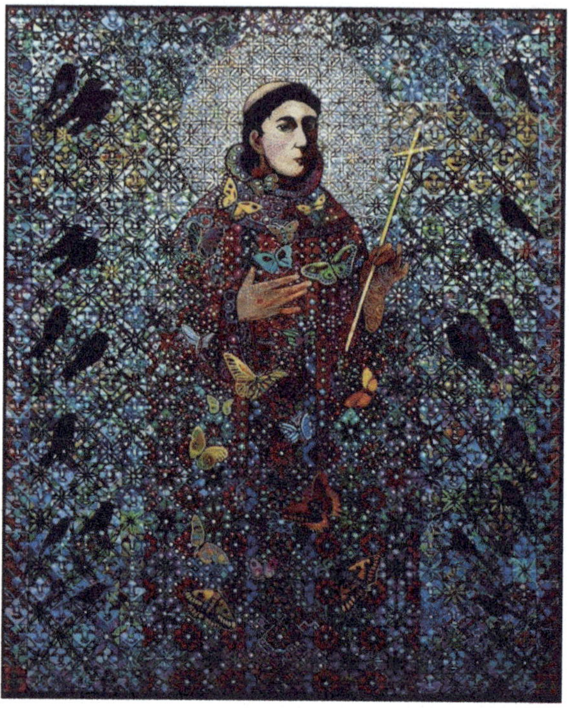

In this painting we only notice a very tiny part of the entire surface: the head. The artist seems to have thought of the rest of the space as completely devoid of significance, except to point to the HEAD. One wonders why he bothered with the rest of the surface at all. Try as you might, there is nothing else to look at, except perhaps for the oversized hand, which unfortunately looks as if it were stuck on as an afterthought. One has to force one to look at anything other than these two objects. It is annoying. One feels managed and manipulated rather than led. The birds are not *painted*, they are *suggested*. The idea is given, not the physical reality, One of the first and most fundamental lessons for the beginning art student is "avoid putting a head in the middle of the page." When we look at this painting, we can see the wisdom in that lesson.

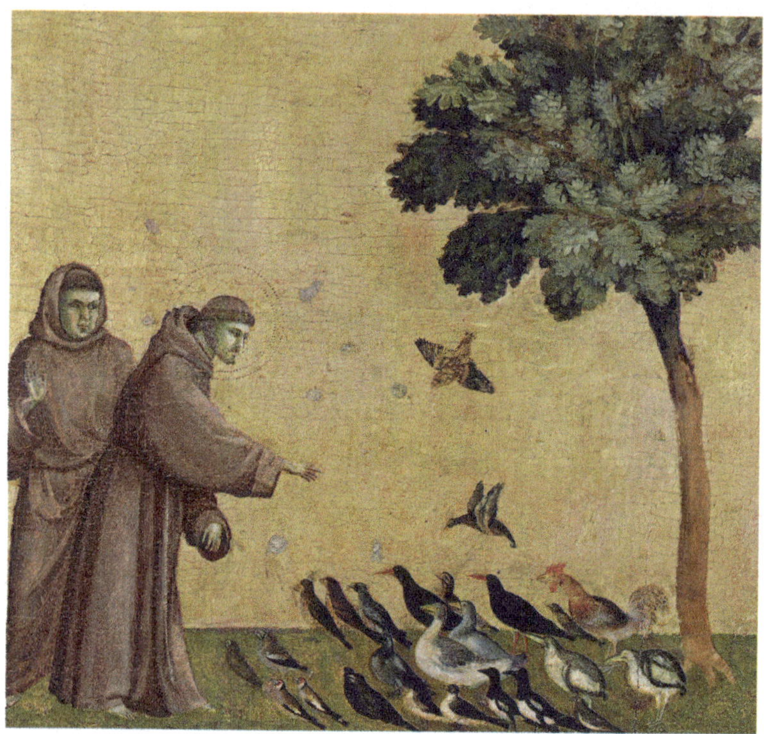

This painting of St. Francis and the birds has a beautiful composition. Immediately when you look at it you see the whole thing. You don't just see St, Francis' face and hand. Your eye is taken all over, Notice how the tree bends towards St. Francis, and the birds pay attention to him. Also notice how the leaves are painted differently than the birds, and how the faces are treated as a part of the composition. The artist did not take advantage of the viewer's probable special interest in the face, which may have tempted him to take shortcuts on the rest of the areas of the painting and to over-emphasize the face, which would have created a sense of unbalance in the whole. The viewer can see that the artist took care with the entirety of the painting.

APPENDIX 9: THE COMPOSITION/INTEGRATION (III)

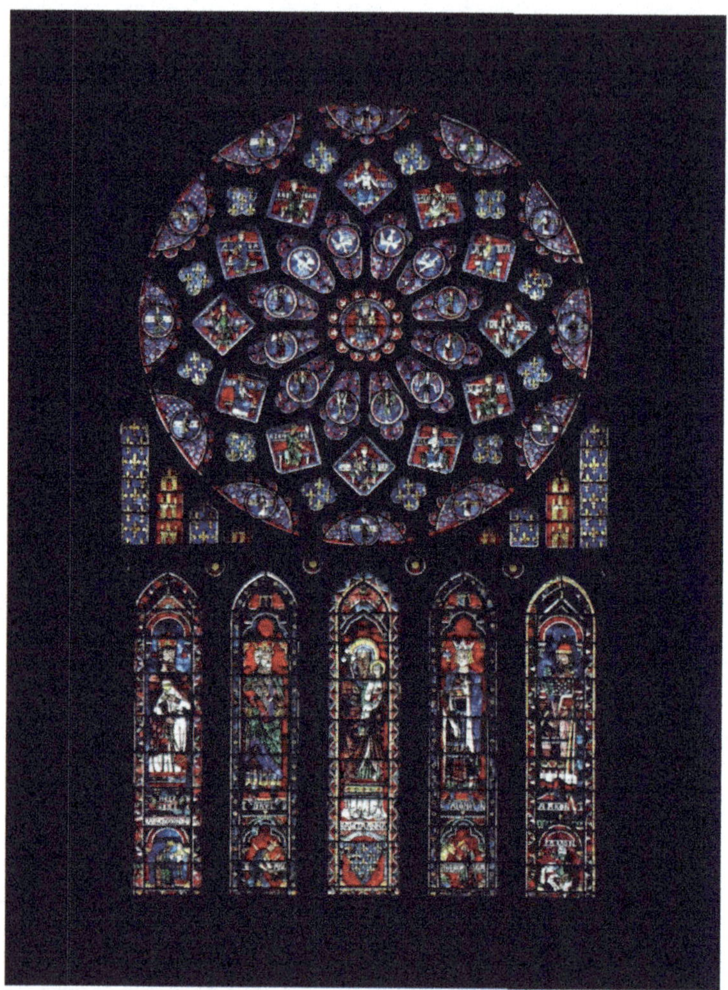

This work of stained glass is one of the most perfect examples of good composition in the history of art. Notice that when you look at it, you cannot see the whole of the subject matter. Notice also that it doesn't matter. The beauty of its design is in itself is completely satisfying.

The process of looking is welcome. The element of 'balance' is perfectly met by the circular form above the strong, straight, pillars. It is balanced because those verticals really look like they can hold up that circle. At the same time there is an element of tension because the shapes are so different: circle and rectangle. Note that the circle is really circular (nothing but a circle can be thought of) and the rectangles are only rectangles (they can only be read as rectangles). One cannot say "Is that supposed to be a rectangle or could it be more of a square?" In other words, an element of good composition is that it is definite. Also note that the circle, which is normally a moving object, is made permanent by being nestled in a series of rectangles which serve as a box, a holder, for the circle. Small objects between the rectangles remind us that that there is no unconsidered emptiness in the universe. After gazing at it for a while, one is drawn to the specifics. One is drawn in. And then what does the viewer experience? A world of stories in pictures! The viewer can study any one of these and sees that each one is in itself another definite composition. In other words, the viewer first experiences that same kind of satisfaction in the design of the specific picture. So, the viewer is drawn in further, to a smaller section. And the same exhilaration strikes him. No matter the level of detail he looks at, the same process - indeed, the creative process--repeats, that of starting with a definite limit and then moving inward, being drawn inward, always having a limit and working within it.

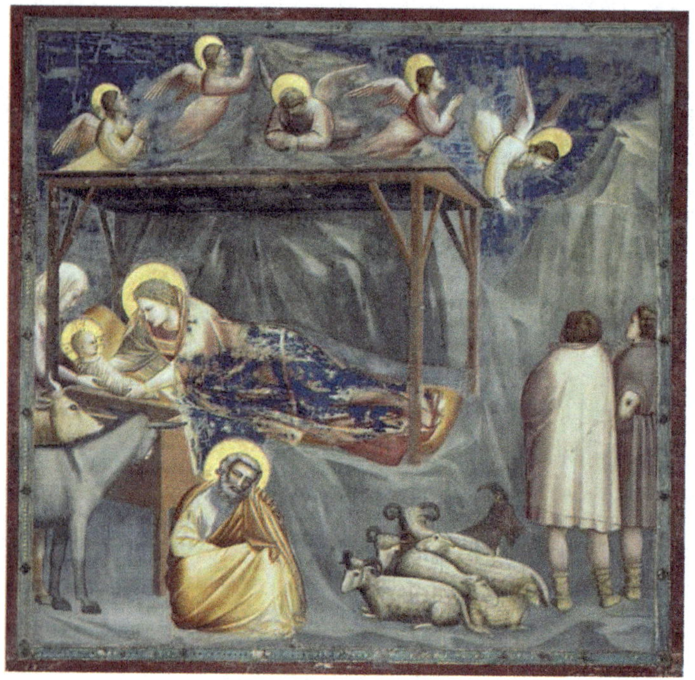

The greatness of the composition in this painting is similar. The viewer takes in the entire painting first, without having the need to immediately 'look for' anything. The eye is directed from any point of interest and is then led around the entire piece. However, when the viewer decides to focus on a small part, he is given an entire new world to contemplate. As in the former stained glass, the painter established a limit (the shape

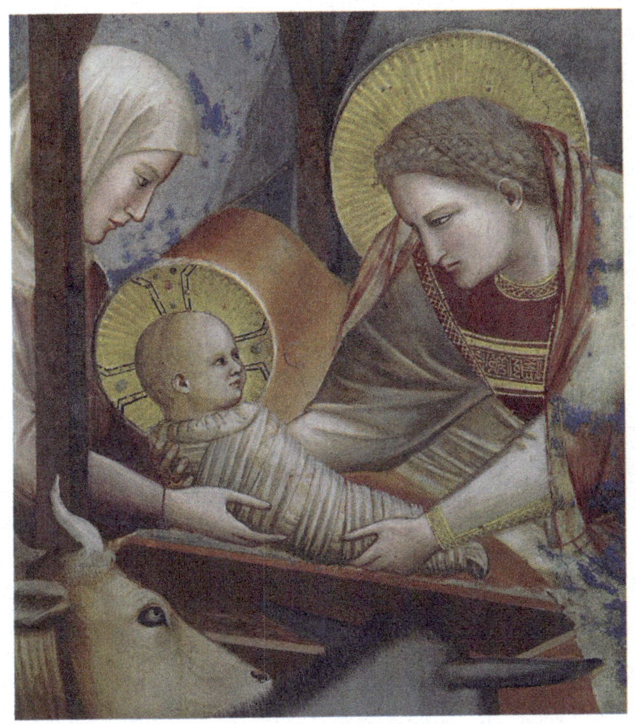

and size of the painting) and worked inward,
inward as much as possible, always making a new
limit and then working within *it*.

APPENDIX 11: THE COMPOSITION/INTEGRATION (V)

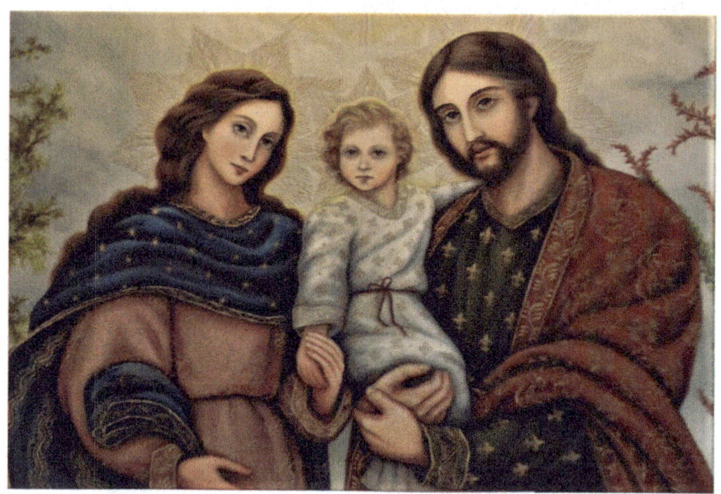

In this painting every part is painted in the same way. The hair and the clothing are both painted with the same method of wavy form, without the sensitivity of the difference between hair and material.

The beard is painted the same way as the skin. Of course, one knows which is which, but the reason that distinction is able to be made has to do with the position and color of each. We do not see diversity and integration developed to a high degree, so we do not experience a *composition*. We are seeing bad composition because the totality of composition is not considered. We are seeing partial composition. In lieu of *integrity*, we see instead a *contraction* of each thing.

The hair is a little less than hair; the material is a little less than material. They have been compressed into something *smaller* than what they are, in order to make them fit together. This is not the way God created the universe. (I selected this work as an example of bad composition, but I must also point out that it is an illustration, not a work of fine art).

The life lesson of this superficial way of looking at composition can be easily translated into behavior: that the path to peace and unity in society is followed through conformity, by our becoming less than what we are, in order to 'get along.' A very dangerous and anti-Catholic lesson.

APPENDIX 12 THE IDEA: THE COMPOSITION/ INTEGRATION (VI)

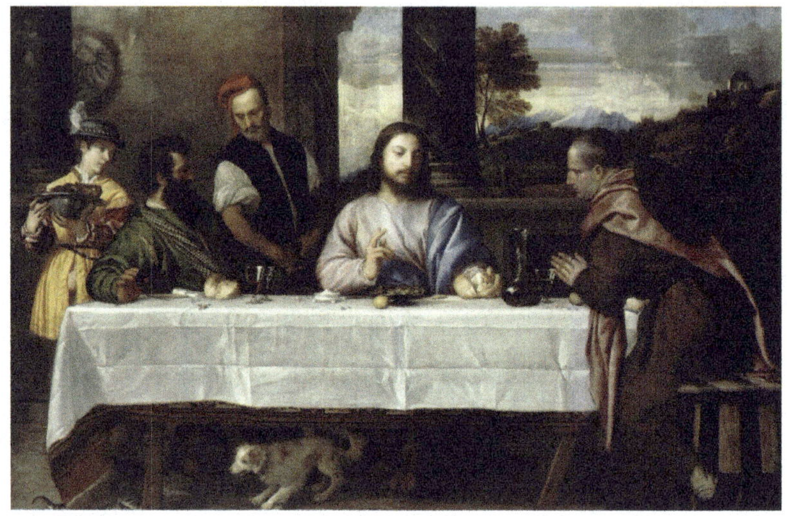

In this painting the artist is aware of the difference in the various materials he is representing. The rough material is painted differently than the satiny, the glass is painted differently than the clouds, the skin is painted differently that the hair. And yet everything makes a whole. Diversity *completely* integrated. That is what makes this a *Composition*. It is a question of respecting and trying to imitate God's created world. And what a lesson for us: that we can be complete individuals, completely different, and yet have an integrated society.

APPENDIX 13 THE IDEA: THE COMPOSITION/ INTEGRATION (VII)

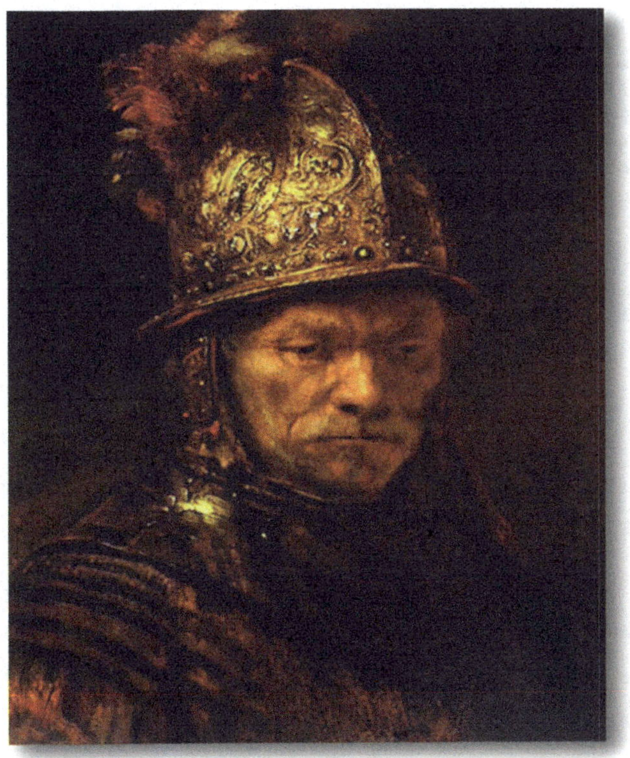

This is another artist who was completely aware of the different qualities of different materials. This also is an example of diversity totally integrated.

Both of these paintings show the beauty of the twin truths of diversity and integration taken as far as the artist was able to take them.

APPENDIX 14 THE IDEA: INTERPRETATION OF THE STORY (I)

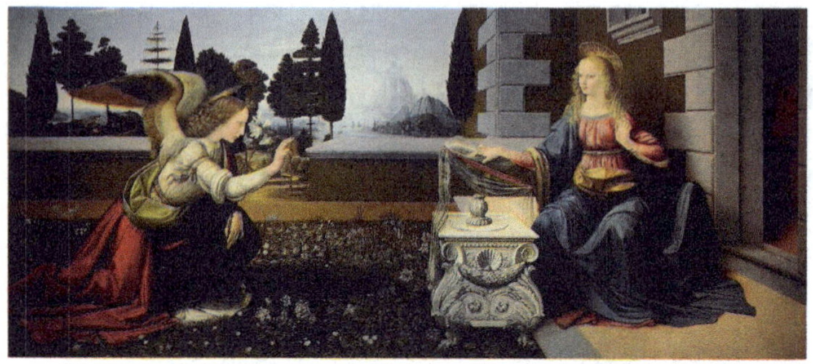

This painting is superlative in just about every area under general criticism except for the Interpretation of the Story. In terms of this part of the idea, this painting is completely unsuccessful. Our Lady was not a rich noblewoman from the Italian Renaissance. Many, if not all, of the paintings from the Renaissance period contain the same error. Our Lady looks as though she is receiving a request from a subject. It represents a misguided attempt at 'improving' on the factual story. Yes, Mary was special, chosen by God. Yes, she became Queen of Heaven and Earth. But she was not special and chosen because she was rich, and she was not queen at the time of the Annunciation. Much has been written about the reasons why artists during this period painted the way they did, but that is art history, not art criticism, and we are concerned with art criticism.

The reason that this is such a major problem is that we are shaped by what we see. For example, it will be difficult to convince a child growing up looking at this type of artwork of the love Jesus has for the poor. The child may be able to recite the fact that the poorest people were the ones first invited to witness His birth, but there will exist inside him a sneaking suspicion that Jesus really prefers the rich, along with the insidious idea that the way to know Jesus loves you is to look at the material aspects of your life. This will be so subtle within him, nothing perhaps he will ever give words to, but will play a big part in shaping his entire attitude to God and society, because this kind of image (more than the actual story) will be what he'll picture when someone mentions the Annunciation. Remember, the artist must stick to the facts.

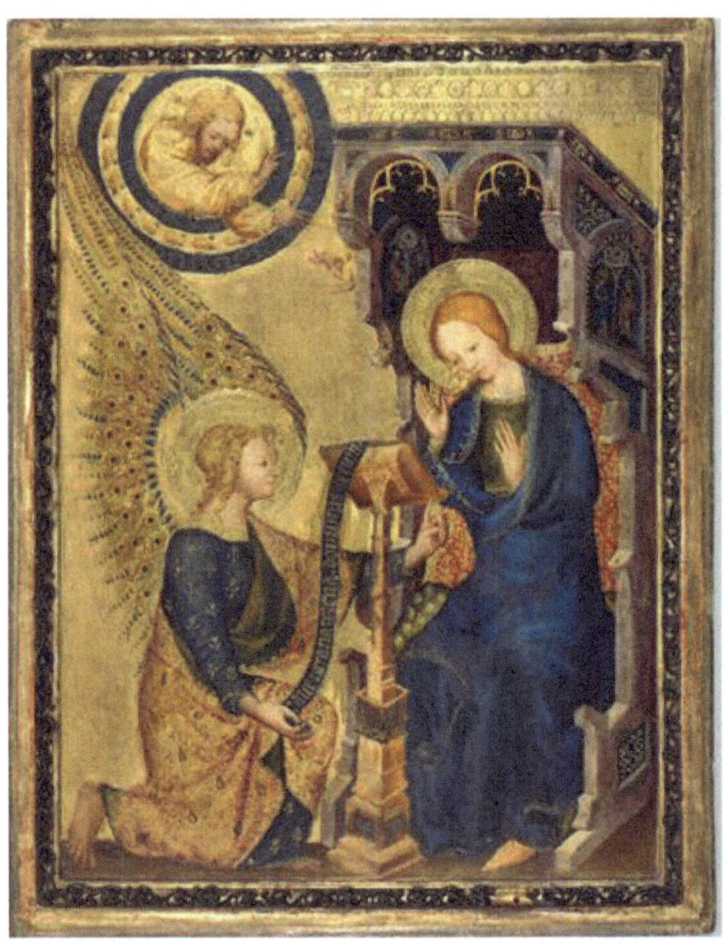

In this painting the Interpretation of the Story is completely successful. All the symbolism is present to deepen our understanding and the figure of Mary is exactly right. She is perfectly holy (the halo), and being honored by God (kneeling angel, who is at the same time in an attitude of attention). We also sense her complete humility, both in her bowed head and in the way her body is covered. Her whole demeanor is one of acquiescence. She seems completely unfocused on herself, but is rather offering herself to God, to use as He sees fit: a message for all of us.

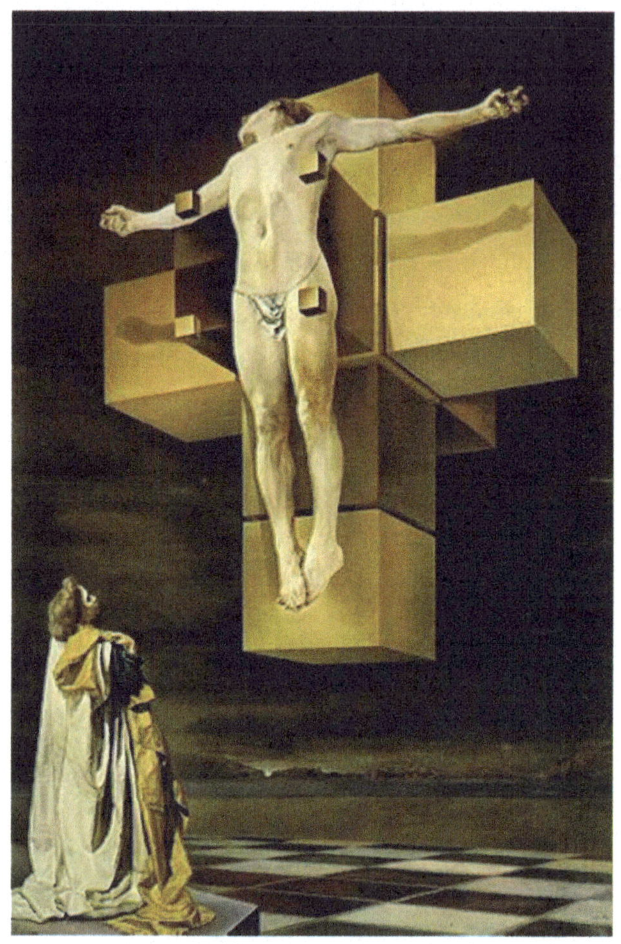

What is the idea of this work? What is the artist saying, what is his statement? It is completely unclear. Is the elevated 'cross' supposed to tell us that movement or impermanence played some part in the crucifixion? Or is the story changed to say that Christ rose at the Crucifixion? We could ask all day. Maybe we'd hit on the right answer or maybe not. Or are we just supposed to feel stupid because we don't immediately 'get it?'

And what do the boxes stuck on His body mean? Since the meaning is unclear I suspect that we are supposed to think that it must have some deep philosophical or psychological meaning. Frankly to me it just looks like a sophomoric show is being put on. It just looks like theater. There is drama but neither horror nor grief. It looks like a diorama, just not a very good one. No transformation is possible through this piece, the message is just too confusing and unsuited to the subject. The crucifixion of Our Lord was a pretty definite thing. The viewer should not have to remain on the level of trying to 'figure it out.' This is a completely unsuccessful interpretation of the crucifixion. Remember, *this is the Crucifixion of Our Lord*. The artist doesn't need to pump it up with cheap theatrics.

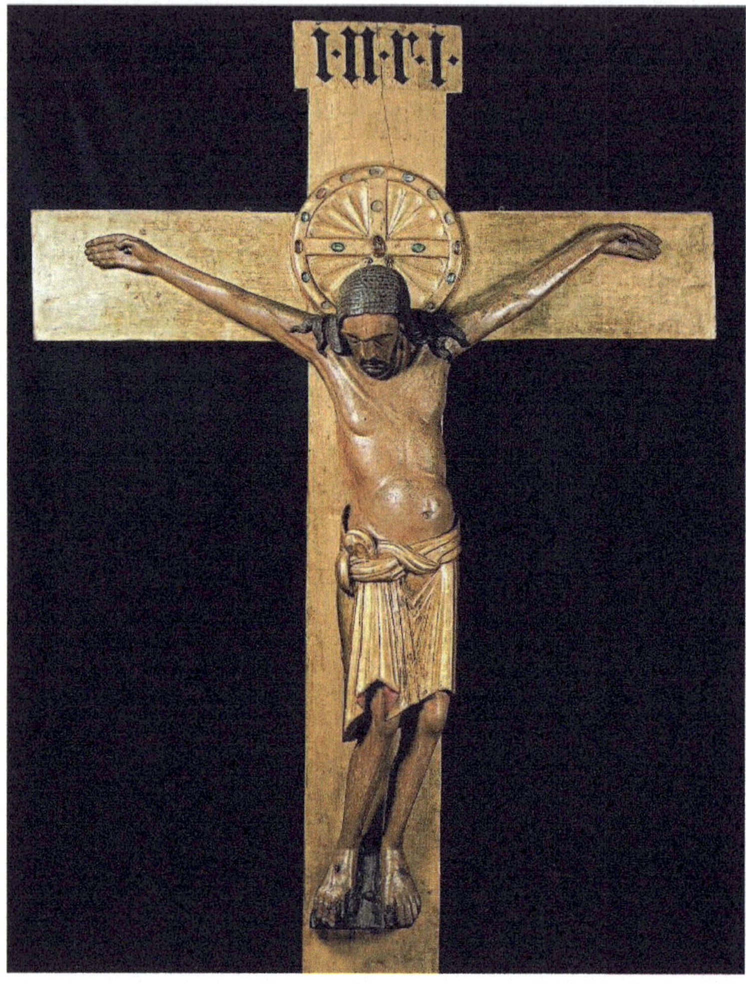

Contrast this statement, this idea, to the previous. The first thing to strike the viewer is the sheer pathos, the strength of which hits the viewer like a tsunami. The idea being expressed in this piece is just that: it is an image so overwhelming in its *definite* depiction of suffering, with such an appeal to both the intellect and the emotions concerning the tragedy shown that there cannot be any question of what the artist is saying. The innocence of the victim is somehow emphasized by the bulging stomach, the stretched skin and the mouth turned down at the corners, all of which serve to underline the human suffering of Our Lord. *We can see Christ suffering and dying for our sins.*

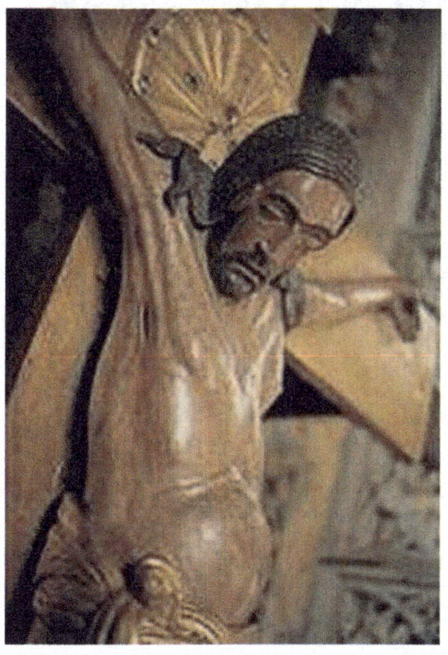

The success of the statement can be understood by the fact that it never occurs to the viewer to ask or wonder what the idea is. What can the viewer do after gazing upon this image except to fall on his knees and be sorry for his sins, which caused it.

APPENDIX 18 THE IDEA: CHOICE OF MEDIUM (I)

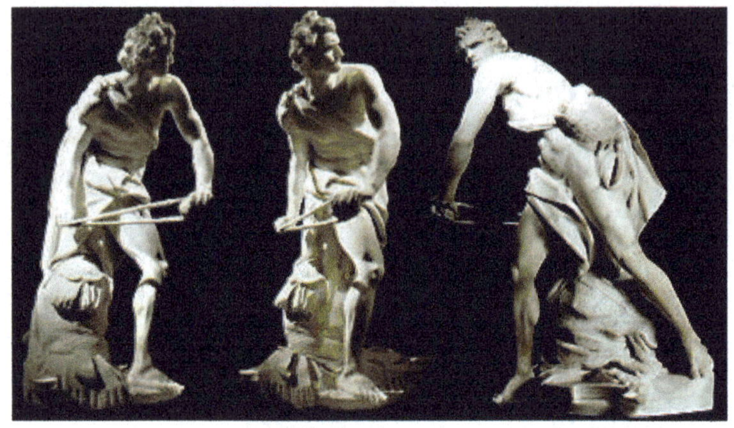

In this marble sculpture the sculptor has not shown any respect for his medium. The major characteristic of stone is its massivity; it exists as a block until broken apart by some violent means. Because of this, stone exudes a sense of strength and permanence, which is why the Church is represented as a Rock. The way that a sculptor understands, respects, and utilizes stone properly is to start with the limits of the block and work inward. Extended limbs and certainly a piece of rope separated from the body have no place in stone carving. Also, notice that the sculptor carved a work that is intended to be seen from every side equally; the viewer is not supposed to recognize a front, sides, or back. He is supposed to walk around. This introduces a sense of movement and impermanence which is completely antithetical to stone. There is lots of 'energy' and 'movement' but it is all going in the wrong direction; it is going outward rather than inward.

The medium is simply not understood by this artist and as a result his idea is confusing.

The message of a sculpture like this is to legitimize getting one's way by the breaking down of barriers, by force or brutality, rather than utilizing creativity to meet challenges. It teaches outward, lateral thinking (non-creativity) over working inward (creative thinking). This cannot be a reflection of the truth; the Church teaches an inner transformation to holiness. This should have been a painting; it's likely that it would have been a masterpiece. As a sculpture, it is simply a failure. Please remember our lesson on technical expertise. This 'sculpture' (really a three dimensional painting) can 'wow', it cannot lead to the truth, simply because the artist has chosen the wrong medium.

This is also a perfect example of an artist asking *"Does it Work."*

He had an 'idea,' something he was trying to 'say.' And this took precedence for him over obeying the limits of his medium (he did not respect his limits).

APPENDIX 19: THE IDEA II: CHOICE OF MEDIUM (II)

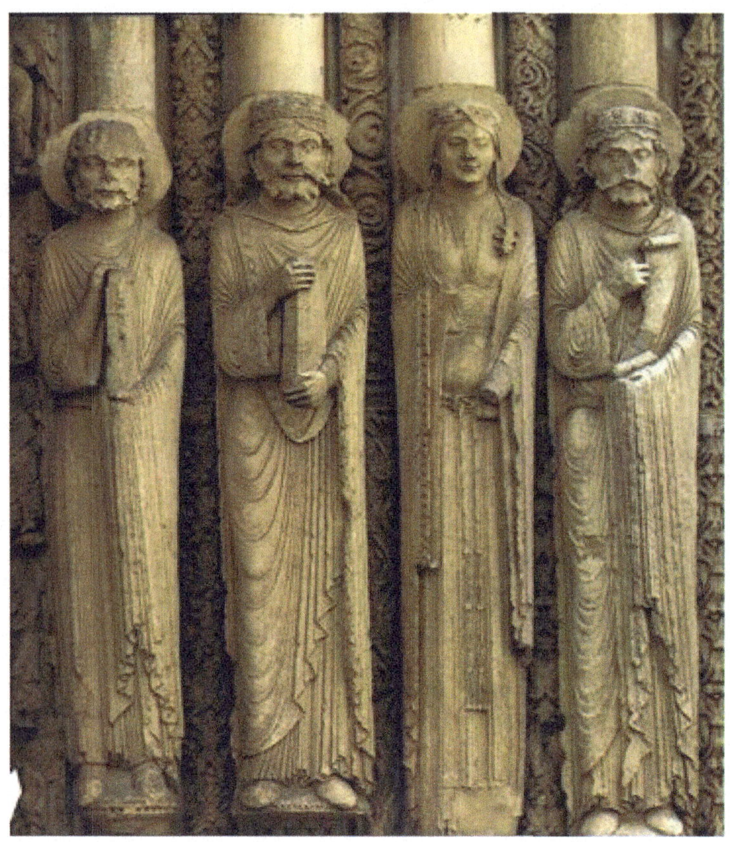

In these carvings we can see that stone was the perfect material to use. We see perfect unity in terms of the idea and the medium. The limit of the shape of the sculptures is emphasized by the pillars we see behind the figures. They seem to be a metamorphosis in action: pillars turning into figures. This 'transitional' quality is noteworthy of good stone sculpture. There is as much 'movement' and 'energy' as in the previous work, but in this case, it is energy in the right direction: inward. These figures exude the atmosphere of stone: permanence and strength. The reason that it is important for the sculptor to respect limits in his work is that *that* becomes a major part of the message: Limits exist and God placed us inside them. The way to God is to work within these limits because working within limits is the act of human creativity. It is repeating the fact that we were made in God's image.

Another way to compare these two stone pieces is to look at the figures themselves. In the first carving the viewer will seem to be aware of what the figure is *doing* rather than who or what he *is*. In the second we are more aware of something *inside* of the figures being expressed.

This is a perfect example of an artist asking *"Is it God's will?"* because he respected the limits of his medium (his limits).

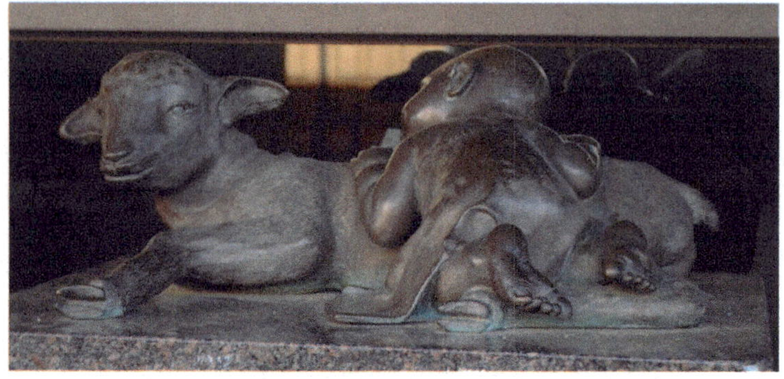

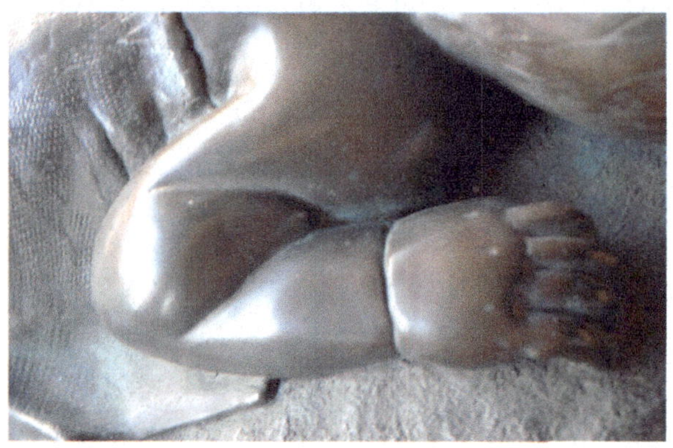

Here we see something very unfortunate; a lovely sculpture ruined due to the lack of technical expertise. The sculptor apparently left the casting of this baby to a foundry and gave up the responsibility to ensure that the casting was done correctly and with care. This arm-and I have chosen just the arm but the entire baby has been done the same way-is a disgrace. Grinders and sanders were used until the forms of the arm were destroyed and 'simplified' into what appears to be a robotic alien. When we think of the folds of a small baby's body and how wonderful they are to observe and we compare it to this we feel nothing but horror. That is, unless we completely disregard the physical and jump over it to our preconceptions of what it is supposed to be, or the 'idea.' If we choose to disregard the physical, however, we cannot be following Christ. The real tragedy of this is that this is an anti-abortion sculpture! An anti-abortion sculpture in which *the physicality of the human child is disregarded.* If the pro-abortion and 'pro-life' people both see the physical human person as an 'idea' and disregard the bodily reality, perhaps this tells us much about the acceptance of abortion in this world.

When we have a society in which people are cast aside in favor of some 'trans-human' robots, let us remember this lesson in the importance of technical expertise.

Note: Sculptors who do not wish to maintain control and responsibility over the *entire* process of sculpture making have no business making sculpture. They must chase their piece *in* the foundry and watch the foundry pour the first mold-making coat. After the casting, they must cut off the sprues at the foundry, take the piece home in to chase it themselves. After this they can take the piece back to have the foundry patina it, if necessary. If the sculptor cannot do this-for whatever reason--he should not be making metal sculpture. Do not work with him: what you see in the model is *not* what you'll get.

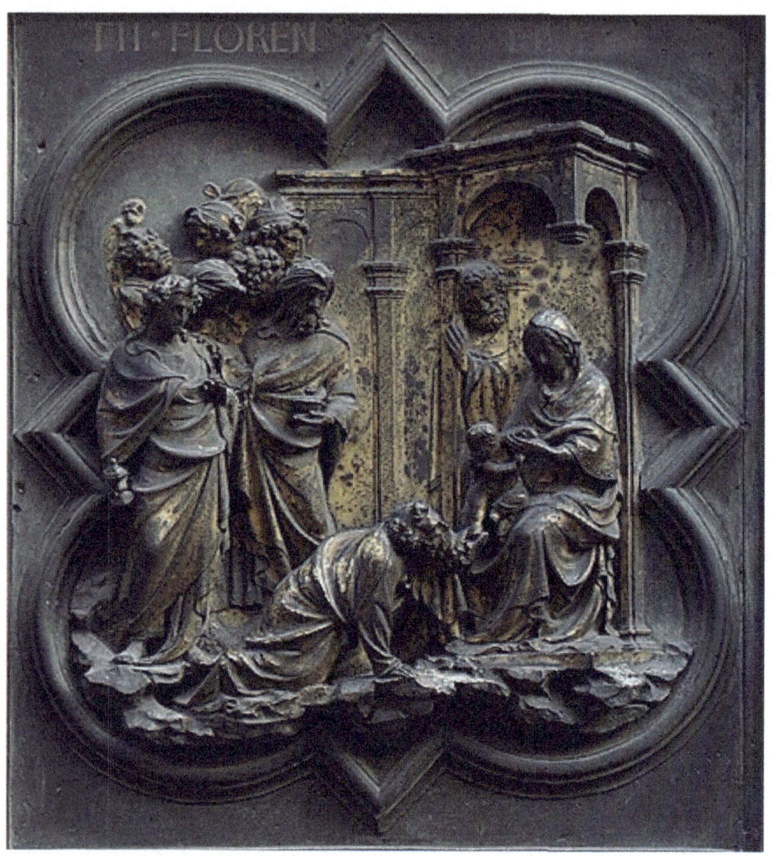

In these bronze reliefs we see what it means when the artist assumes full control over the technical aspect of the work. When these works were made, no foundry was satisfactory to the artist so he set up his own foundry and employed family members to run it. The beauty and the detail could only be possible when the artist supervised every aspect of the casting process of his own work. To have real artistic value, bronze sculpture, as well as any other art form, must bear the original mark of the artist. This makes for communication between artist and viewer, and makes possible a journey taken together that goes *through* the physical to the spiritual. This is the soil that may predispose the viewer that there is such a thing as truth.

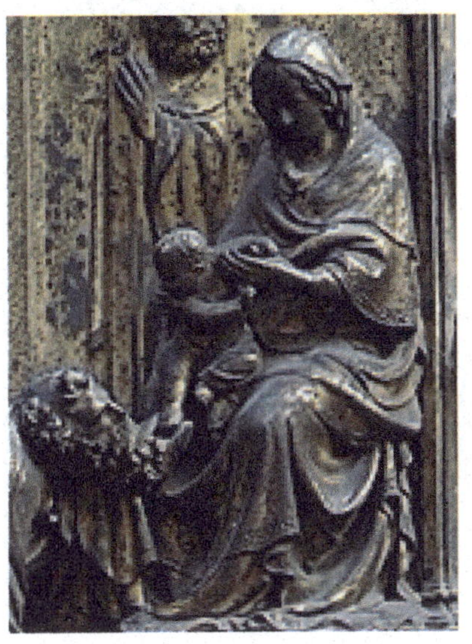

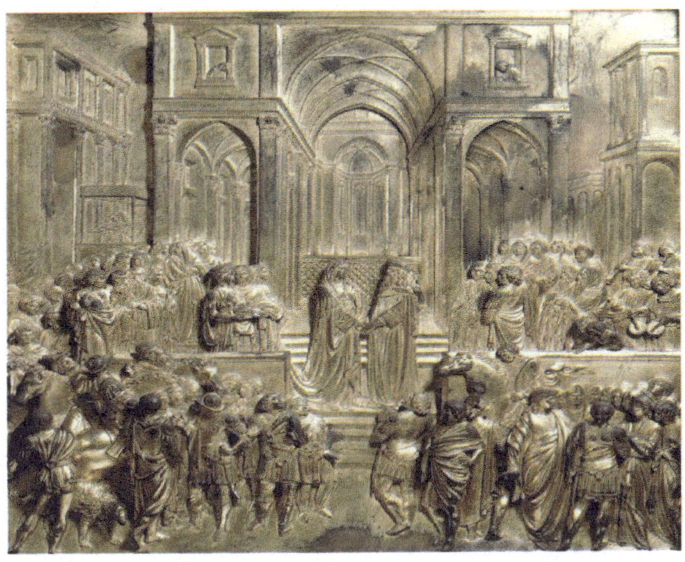

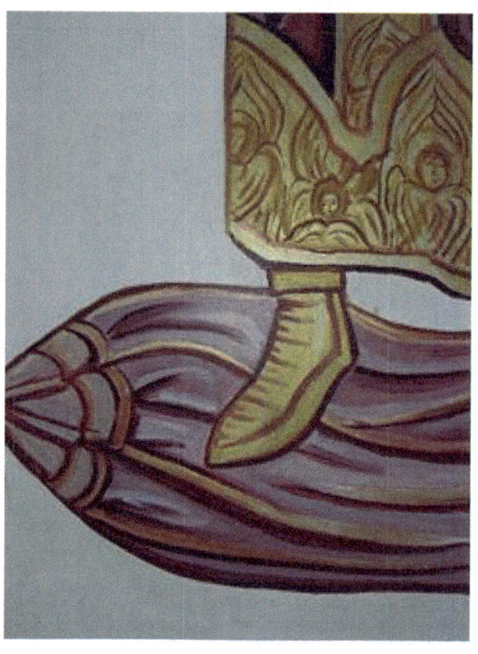

This detail of the foot shows absolutely no sense of development, of decisions being considered, then chosen and executed with thought and care. Every mark looks mechanical and thoughtless. Every mark looks as though the painter put down the first casual thought that entered his head and then walked away. It shows absolutely no respect for the created world. Among the thoughts not considered: *Which foot is this supposed to be, the right or the left? What is essential about a foot-its form, its line, its beauty, its purpose, its relationship to the body, what it's holding up, what it's standing on? And which of these do I want to focus on in order for this foot*

to be a substantial part of the whole painting, my whole statement? This thoughtless, amateurish, almost embarrassingly undeveloped excuse for "art" is not only painful to look at, but carries with it some very serious negative lessons that have no place in a Catholic Church. These lessons are: First of all, forget trying to teach a child (or anyone else) Matthew 10:29-30: *"Are not two sparrows sold for a small coin? Yet not one of them falls to the ground without your Father's knowledge. Even all the hairs of your head are counted."* Secondly, don't try to teach a child how to write an essay, that it must have an introduction, a supportive body, and then a conclusion. In fact, don't be surprised when the society as a whole abandons the creative process altogether and completely forgets what it means to have been created in God's image. Images like this, inside of a church building, can take a good deal of the credit.

Appendix 23: The Development of the Work II)

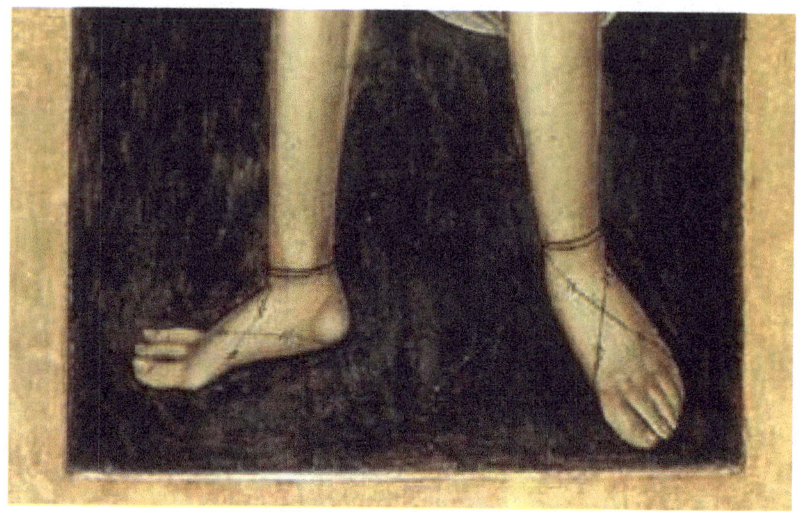

In this painting of feet, we can see the exact opposite of theprevious attempt. We sense, see and can feel the journey, or the development of the artist in terms of how to paint feet. There is the obvious-that the artist actually gave thought to the structure and purpose of a foot. Then there is the anatomical knowledge-we can see musculature, the difference of weight placed on each foot, the care present in the painting of the toes, even the spaces between the toes. The sensitivity to how straps would wind around the various parts of the feet is a pleasure to look at. In every part we feel the respect this artist has for all of God's creation, even something as small as the feet, as a toe, and yes, even a toenail. It is important him to pay attention to everything; in this he is trying to imitate God, and in so doing he is glorifying God.

He is teaching us something vital; he is taking us through nature to a truth about the universe. It is difficult to study this exquisite little detail and walk away unchanged.

Such is the purpose of fine art.

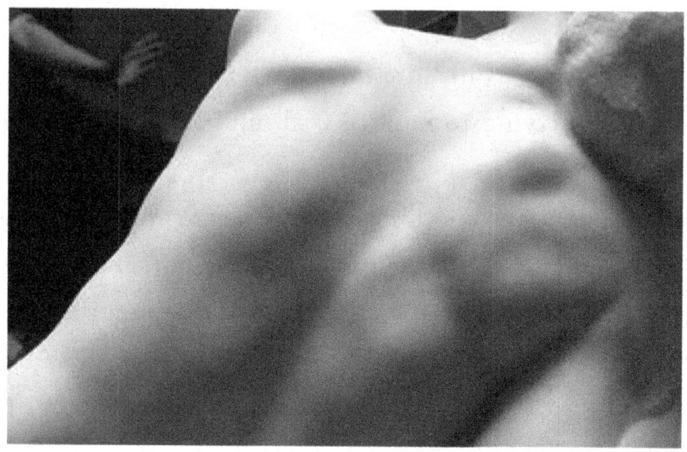

In this marble sculpture we can see an extremely weak conclusion. There is lack of clarity in the forms of the back. In this case it is due to the fact that abrasives were used to smooth out the surface of the marble. It looks 'finished' but the finished look comes from seeing that the surface cannot be made any smoother, not because of any decision of the sculptor. The 'forms' of the back could be a back; on the other hand, they could be a sand dune if they weren't attached to a head. It looks like a challenge unmet. This problem of the lack of a strong conclusion teaches the viewer that the 'process' is all there is, that there is nothing at the end. A diet of this kind of work helps to ensure that people disregard the four final things.

APPENDIX 25: THE CONCLUSION OF THE WORK (II)

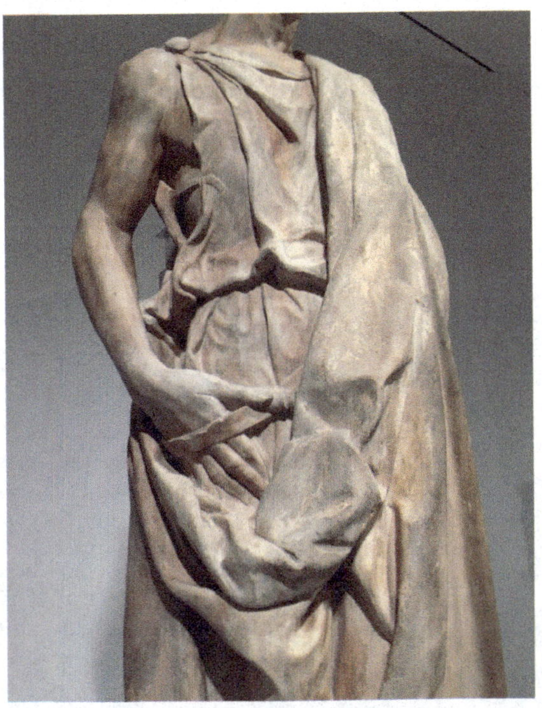

In this piece the sculptor has made real and concrete decisions about every form. No mushed and smoothed out 'forms' here. There is no guesswork in terms of what each form represents. This sculptor has made every form distinct, developed and *finished*. He knew exactly what he wanted to do and did it. No form could have been taken any farther. He did not begin something and then peter out. He took responsibility for his actions; he *finished* it. It is finished. What a tremendous lesson! How we should pray that these can be *our* last words!

APPENDIX 22: HOMEWORK ASSIGNMENT

These are the reliefs done by the two finalists for the commission for the bronze Baptistry doors in Florence, Italy, 1401. Which would you have chosen, and why? Remember, begin with the composition and go through all of the characteristics studied. (Hint: The judges made the correct decision. Can you explain why)?

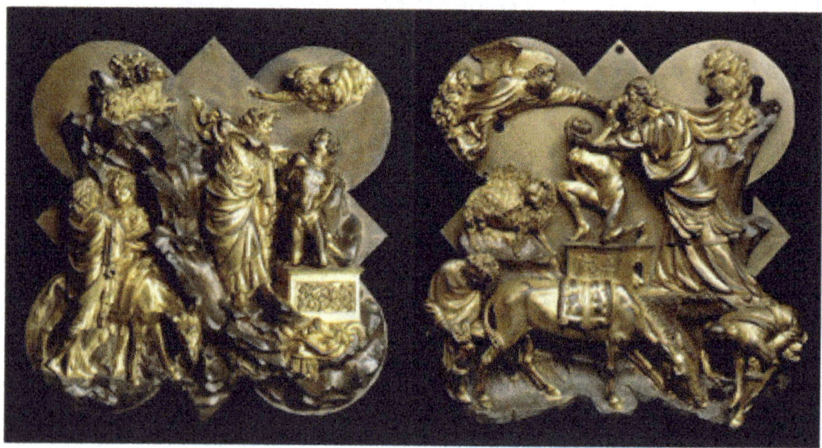

NOTES

<u>**NOTES**</u>

<u>**Suggested Further Reading**</u>

1. ***On the Holy Icons***, St. Theodore the Studite

2. ***Three Treatises on the Divine Images,*** St. John of Damascus

3. ***Christ and Apollo: The Dimensions of the Literary Imagination***, William F. Lynch, S.J.

   Although this focuses on literature it is extremely valuable as an approach to the visual arts as well.

4. ***The Mind of the Maker,*** Dorothy Sayers

   Keep in mind that the author was not a Catholic. Still, it presents a description of the relationship of Trinitarian Reality to the human creative process which is well worth reading; also with an emphasis on literature.

5. ***The Natural Way to Draw,*** Kimon Nicolaides

   This book enables you to teach yourself how to draw. It is absolutely the best book available that I know for this.

The author is organizing a course on Art Criticism expanding on the material covered in this book.

Anyone interested in more information on this course should contact the author:

theprofaneinsacredart@yahoo.com

ABOUT THE AUTHOR

Kathleen Whittaker was born in Pennsylvania, U.S.A. She was educated at the New York Studio School of Drawing, Painting and Sculpture and at the Philadelphia College of Art. She also studied independently in Florence, Italy. She developed a unique method of figurative stone carving in Portugal, where she lived for nearly twenty years. She has public sculptures in Portugal, France, Ireland and the United States.

She currently lives in Arizona, U.S.A.

Made in the USA
Columbia, SC
21 November 2022

71200872R00104